MODELLING THE GROWTH OF CORPORATIONS

Also by Michèle Sanglier

COMPLEXITY AND SELF-ORGANISATION IN SOCIAL AND ECONOMIC SITUATIONS (*with Fukang Fang*)

Also by Paul Brenton

GLOBAL TRADE AND EUROPEAN WORKERS (*edited with Jacques Pelkmans*)
INTERNATIONAL TRADE: A EUROPEAN TEXT (*with Henry Scott and Peter Sinclair*)

Modelling the Growth of Corporations

Applications for Managerial Techniques and Portfolio Analysis

Jacques Solvay
Michèle Sanglier
and
Paul Brenton

Foreword by Ilya Prigogine

palgrave

First published 2001 by
PALGRAVE
Houndmills, Basingstoke, Hampshire RG21 6XS and
175 Fifth Avenue, New York, N.Y. 10010
Companies and representatives throughout the world

PALGRAVE is the new global academic imprint of
St. Martin's Press LLC Scholarly and Reference Division and Palgrave
Publishers Ltd (formerly Macmillan Press Ltd).

ISBN 0–333–94642–1

This book is printed on paper suitable for recycling and made from fully managed and sustained forest sources.

A catalogue record for this book is available from the British Library.

Library of Congress Cataloging-in-Publication Data

Solvay, Jacques, 1920–
    Modelling the growth of corporations: applications for managerial techniques and portfolio analysis / by Jacques Solvay, Michele Sanglier, and Paul Brenton.
        p. cm.
    Includes bibliographical references and index.
    ISBN 0–333–94642–1
        1. Corporations—Growth—Econometric models.
        2. Corporations—Valuation—Econometric models. 3. Investment analysis. I. Title: Modeling the growth of corporations.
        II. Sanglier, M. III. Brenton, Paul. IV. Title.
HD2746 .S65 2001
658.15—dc21
                                                                              2001032792

10   9   8   7   6   5   4   3   2   1
10   09 08 07 06 05 04 03 02 01

Printed and bound in Great Britain by
Antony Rowe Ltd, Chippenham, Wiltshire

Contents

List of Figures

List of Tables and Boxes

Tables

Boxes

Foreword

It is a privilege and a pleasure to write a few words on the occasion of the publication of this book by Jacques Solvay, Michèle Sanglier and Paul Brenton on *Modelling the Growth of Corporations*. I have known Jacques Solvay for many years. I must say that he is an extraordinary person. Jacques is a direct descendant of Ernest Solvay, the founder of one of the most important world chemicals companies. In parallel to his action as inventor and industrialist, Ernest Solvay had a deep interest in the sciences, in physics, chemistry, physiology and sociology. At the beginning of the last century he founded what is now called the International Institutes in Physics and Chemistry in Brussels and started the series of Solvay symposia which had a decisive influence on the history of physics and chemistry in the last century.

Jacques Solvay shares the interests of his great grandfather. He was Chairman of Solvay Industries for twenty years and has been Chairman of the Administrative Council of the International Institutes for Physics and Chemistry, where I have been Director since 1958. I have had the privilege to collaborate closely with Jacques Solvay over all of these years. Sometimes it was a curious situation; on the one side Jacques Solvay was a Chairman but was often behaving more like a research fellow, especially when our research into non-equilibrium physics came to interest sociologists and economists. I am very happy that the present book is the fruit of long years of collaboration between Jacques Solvay and the Institutes.

Everybody agrees that with the new century we come close to a bifurcation point, facing new challenges in a world subject to substantial change. How, for example, will we be able to apprehend the emerging complexity of the new communications-based networks, which imply new forms of relationships between individuals, illustrated in part by the phenomenon of the 'World Wide Web'?

In all aspects of our modern life, new structures, social and economic, appear and change, adapt and possibly disappear, more and more quickly. In this world where managers, politicians and decision-makers in companies face the same challenge, that is to think differently or in other ways, it is indeed more than ever necessary to reconsider our vision of the world. In particular we need to take into account the limited cognitive abilities or bounded rationality of the economic actor who interacts with his or her environment on the basis of new dialogues. Both are parts of the same problem, both are influenced by, and have influence upon, the decisions of the individual and the interpretation of their consequences (feedback effects).

It is necessary, then, for us to analyse the problems that we face using new methods, based in particular upon recognition of the role of uncertainty in the emergence of new organisations which are generated, sustained and modified, according to complex and irreversible dynamic processes. Non-linearities and dynamic reactions lead to 'non-equilibrium' outcomes. In all fields of knowledge, we have to replace the classical views based on determinism and time reversibility by a probabilistic view. The role of contingency is evident in human history and especially in fields such as economics.

Most approaches to economics stem from ideas that are centuries old-dominated by the seventeenth-century cognitive frameworks of René Descartes and Isaac Newton. The remarkable success of those frameworks in explaining and predicting the behaviour of physical systems provided the foundation of modern science and engineering and of 'industrial age' businesses. These approaches describe systems at or close to, equilibrium and are still popular.

However, there are increasingly obvious limits to what this 'mechanical' approach can do, because it was conceived to explain systems consisting of stable parts operating according to fixed physical rules. Such systems ignore the effects of learning, evolution, or changes in those rules. The Cartesian perspective of inanimate objects and the forces acting on them is not suited to inquiries about biological and social systems. Unlike simple mechanical systems, they learn, they adapt, and they evolve. Living systems, including all human activities, are far from equilibrium.

This underlines the need for new evolutionary approaches based, on the one hand, on the recognition of our incapacity to predict everything with accuracy and, on the other hand, on new definitions for economic actors with bounded rationality. In this context, solutions driven by multidisciplinary models enlighten us more about the inner interactions of the model being considered, rather than prediction. In this way, the future that emerges will be only one of a range of possible outcomes represented by these solutions. The laws that we can formulate can define only possibilities, never certainties.

The complexity approach looks at how evolving systems function and adapt. Human complex adaptive systems have the distinguishing characteristic of carrying out socially coordinated activities. Social systems typically comprise multiple interacting units, and are characterised by the emergence and evolution of a nested hierarchical organisation and structure. Further, social systems are composed of individuals each being capable of learning and adaptation as a result of their experiences. The activities that these individuals carry out require a mindset and language that goes beyond the mechanical and that includes learning and ideas. Human decisions involve memory of the past and anticipations of the future.

I understand that there are two complementary processes in corporations. The first is familiar to everyone: instrumental or operational processes, the world of 'doing'. This consists of the routines and behaviours that produce things, create value, improve efficiency, and satisfy needs. They remain largely a mechanical world, and they work well that way. The other part is less familiar and is often not emphasised: organisational (not individual) entrepreneurial processes, the world of collectively shared ideas. This is the source of novelty and innovation and is, in a very real sense, the foundation for the sustainable success of an organisation. It is the cognitive basis for the organisation.

In the 'industrial age', we dealt with a slowly changing environment and the emphasis was on operations and development of infrastructures to carry out well-defined processes. Today the requirement has shifted to flexibility, adaptation, robustness, and speed. Enterprises are guided and tied together by ideas, by their knowledge of themselves and of what they do and can accomplish. Cognitive infrastructures, not physical infrastructures, now determine long-term business success.

Within this framework, it is always with pleasure that I read works directed towards the dynamic analysis of interactions between actors in the social and economic fields and in particular the work presented here by Jacques Solvay and his collaborators. Whilst demonstrating that the corporation is typically driven along a natural exponential growth path, the authors draw attention to some fundamental features inherent to human behaviour, and the implications for the modelling and understanding of complex adaptive systems such as firms. Sustained growth results as one successful strategy, among others, for a human co-operative organisation seeking to survive in a complex economic environment. The authors argue clearly that in the modern complex, self-organising firm the key to long-term success lies in providing an environment in which learning and new ideas flourish, in short corporate culture is crucial.

The model presented here by the authors is an interesting illustration of applications that can be derived from approaches based upon complexity. In addition, this work also provides a practical demonstration that corporations may benefit from analysing their structure as complex, evolving and adaptive systems. It is learning processes and the generation and application of new ideas that defines which, out of many, future paths the firm will follow.

At the start of this foreword, I mentioned the active interest and participation of Jacques Solvay in the scientific team developed by the Solvay Institutes. One of the contributions of the Institutes has been the creation of the *Cellule de Modélisation de la Complexité en Sciences Sociales*. Professor Michèle Sanglier has been a leading member of this group for many years. She is the author of numerous of publications especially in the field of the 'spatial economy'. Paul Brenton is Senior Research Fellow at the Centre for European Policy Studies in Brussels. He has written widely on economic issues, with a particular focus on international trade and foreign direct investment.

Understanding how corporations develop is a key element in the appreciation of the future of economics. For this reason, I am convinced that this monograph will be of great interest to a wide range of readers.

ILYA PRIGOGINE
Nobel Laureate in Chemistry
Director of the International Institutes for Physics and Chemistry
founded by Ernest Solvay, Brussels, and Centre for Studies in Statistical
Mechanics and Complex Systems, University of Texas, Austin, Texas

Acknowledgements

We are most grateful to Jenny Campion, Claude Loutrel and Marc Romain for their contributions to this book and the ideas that it contains.

The authors and publishers would like to thank Elsevier Science for kind permission to reproduce material previously published in the *International Business Review*, vol. 7, 1998, 463–81.

J. S.
M. S.
P. B.

1 Introduction: Modern Economic and Corporate Growth

1.1 GENERAL INTRODUCTION

Consistent growth of income and of living standards is a feature of modern industrial economies. One of the 'stylised facts' concerning growth, first discussed by Kaldor in 1961[1] but equally pertinent today, is that output per worker has continually risen 'at a steady trend rate' over a long period of time and has shown no tendency to decline. This book is concerned with understanding and modelling economic growth. However, unlike much of the economic literature we concentrate on analysing the growth of productivity of the corporation. Just as the productivity of nations has grown consistently, so too has the output per person employed in the typical modern large corporation. But, as at the national level, it is clear that different corporations grow at different rates over fairly long periods of time. This book develops an approach for understanding and modelling the productivity growth of individual corporations.

The simple empirical approach that is developed allows for a comparison between the growth performance of different corporations operating in the same market and shows how study of this feature is helpful in evaluating management strategies and in assessing the performance of firms before and after a merger. The book then proceeds to demonstrate how the growth of productivity is strongly linked with the growth of the profitability of the corporation and, in turn, with the stock market valuation of the company. This analysis can be used as an important piece of information in making long-term portfolio investment decisions. The book has been written so as to be amenable to all who are interested in understanding the growth of corporate productivity whether they be analysts, managers within industry or those making decisions on how to allocate portfolio investment funds between different corporations. Throughout technical details are kept to a minimum in the text and detailed technical explanations are provided in appendixes in chapter 3 for those who

1

wish to explore them, but they are never necessary for further progress in the book.

Many of the features of modern-day corporate growth are difficult to reconcile with the traditional economic theory of the firm in which the emphasis remains on equilibrium or stable outcomes. The approach in this book is based upon a more modern view of the corporation as a complex, evolving organisation. A key feature is that of *self-organisation*, whereby the system or structure of the firm changes in response to accumulated experience and the environment in which it exists. The book shows that continuous growth is the outcome of this evolving process within the modern corporation and that the environment or culture that exists within the firm determines the magnitude of growth. The main force or fuel for steady growth of productivity is technological change and experience and learning processes which are embodied in individual workers.

In this first chapter we provide a brief background to the material which follows in the rest of the book. We start by providing an overview of the growth of industrial countries and the key role played by technology in the process of productivity growth. We then discuss the importance of understanding corporate growth and the key features of the view of the corporation which underlies the approach adopted in the book. Finally, we provide a short summary of each of the chapters which follow.

1.2   MODERN ECONOMIC GROWTH

Modern industrial countries enjoy seemingly endless growth in living standards. The sustained increase in living standards, defined as modern economic growth by Kuznets,[2] is, however, a recent manifestation in economic history. Prior to 1780, when modern economic growth is generally deemed to have started in Britain and then subsequently in the USA and mainland Europe, living standards remained fairly constant for over five centuries and all major civilisations had similar standards of living. In this earlier period there were times when the amount of goods and services produced in a country grew but subsequently population increased, with the effect that living standards changed little. This interaction between population and living standards lies at the heart of the Malthusian model of income determination.

However, since the beginning of the nineteenth century the predictions of Malthus have not come to fruition in the now-industrialised countries. Populations did grow, but not to the extent that they swamped the rising levels of income, enabling *per capita* incomes to grow steadily. The increase in material wealth over the nineteenth and twentieth centuries has been phenomenal compared with previous periods of history. In the USA and Europe living standards over the past 120 years have risen by factors of around 10. Improvements in living standards, as conventionally measured by economists, reflect rising levels of output or production per person, which is commonly known as 'increasing productivity'. At the heart of this sustained leap in living standards lies the introduction and application of new technologies and the accumulation of human capital, reflecting the level of skill, education and training embodied in an individual.

1.3 THE GROWTH OF COMPANIES

The increase in productivity that we observe for industrial nations is the result of the growth of individual companies. In the modern industrial economy the dominant mode of organising and producing output is the corporation. This book is primarily concerned with understanding the growth of corporate productivity. The underlying paradigm is one where firms are not identical, corporate culture matters, and there are differences between corporations in the extent to which they develop and exploit existing and new technologies. We show that just as at the national level growth appears to occur at a fairly constant rate so, too, at the corporate level productivity grows exponentially over medium-term periods. We develop a simple model which can explain this feature and which allows us to analyse and compare the performance of firms within and across markets. This means that the model can be useful as a management tool to analyse the implications of different firm strategies. The model can be very simply applied to available data from company accounts using simple tools in spreadsheets.

The key element in the approach we develop here, as in most models of economic growth, is technological advancement. However, much of the economic literature on growth concentrates upon national productivity growth and pays little attention to corporate growth. In other words, most attention has been given to the macroeconomics of growth rather than the microeconomic factors which underpin the growth of national economies. This reflects in part the assumptions that underlie standard economic analysis, that firms are identical and that those who work in these firms behave in an identical rational way. This standard economic approach proves to be sterile as an explanation of the growth processes exhibited by modern corporations.

1.4 CORPORATE CULTURE AND THE BOUNDED RATIONALITY OF THE INDIVIDUAL

A major feature which underlies the approach in this book is the way in which behaviour within the firm is treated. The particular view of the firm is derived from extensive experience of the way that large corporations operate, evolve and grow and from theories of 'dissipative structures', owing to the insights of Ilya Prigogine,[3] which stress the 'self-organising' features of organisations of individuals such as firms. In short, the corporation is seen as an evolving complex system in a dynamic world in which the process of self-organisation entails a process of adaptation based upon learning and experience and upon changes to the external environment. Key elements in this view of the firm are that the history of a company plays an integral role in determining its future evolution and growth and that the ethics and corporate culture within an enterprise are important. A vital process within the firm is that of *learning* and the *transmission of information* derived from the learning process to others in the firm. This in turn is determined by the nature of the institution that is the firm and the way that relationships are organised within that institution. Learning processes ensure that over time productivity rises as the effectiveness with which a given technology is applied increases. Equally pertinent, just as research and development (R&D) leads to the development of new products and processes so information from those applying and using existing technologies demonstrates the scope for new technological advancements. The firm operates in an environment in which new potentials and new possibilities are being continually created. Improvements are always possible, and in practice are implemented regularly.

To be more specific, it is changes in technology which are translated by firms into higher productivity. Technological change is forever pushing out the boundaries of the productive potential of the enterprise. However, the magnitude of this effect for a given level of investment in technology is a function of the corporate culture of the enterprise. Within the firm, the growth of an individual's productive potential is determined by the way in which they draw upon the technical experience and knowledge acquired by all of the agents working in an enterprise. This is determined by their motivation, education, training, the general environment in which they work and the way that they interact with other individuals within the firm. An implication of this is that there will be differences between corporations in the effectiveness with which new technological opportunities and the existing stock of knowledge are translated into actual increments in productivity and, consistent with what we observe, that corporations grow at different rates.

The underlying view of the individual is quite different from that of the normal economic approach. In mainstream economics, the individual is taken to be completely rational that is, the individual is able to process all of the available and relevant information so as always to choose the optimal and most efficient courses of action. This view demands a great deal of human behaviour and is really useful only in providing solutions to theoretical economic problems. Kenneth Arrow[4] suggests that the individual in this neo-classical economic tradition is a 'lightning calculator'.

More realistically, this book assumes that individuals have bounded rationality and that in seeking to solve the complicated processes that face them their knowledge or cognitive resources is limited. Thus, the individual seeks to interpret, to learn and to adapt to the problems that they face. The way that individuals react is determined by their experience and the nature of social relations and the institutions in which they operate. The way that the firm evolves is dependent upon the way that individuals within the firm interact and, in particular, in the way that the individual draws upon the accumulated experience which is embodied in all of the agents working in the enterprise.

1.5 THE BOUNDARY OF THE FIRM

The view here is one where the boundaries, and the size, of the firm are continually being extended by new technological opportunities and are not limited by rising production costs as in traditional economic models. Traditional economics has little to say about the growth of productivity within large corporations. Yet large firms dominate the industrial landscape. Large corporations are also much more complex than in the standard economic approach to the firm in the ways outlined above. Constraints upon the expansion of the firm arise from lack of effective internal coordination between individuals within the firm which limits the learning processes and constrains the impact on productivity of applying new technologies.

In the traditional neo-classical economic model of national growth, which dominated economic thinking from the 1950s through to the end of the 1990s, the long-run rate of growth of output per worker is determined by the rate of technological progress, which is treated as being exogenous. The most frequently used analogy for this economic view was that technical progress descended like manna from heaven and that there was little that countries could do to affect their long-run growth rate.

More recently, a revolution has occurred in the economic approach to growth with the development of the often-cited *endogenous growth theory*, which follows from the initial ideas of Paul Romer's. For Romer, the key driving force behind technological progress is explicit investment in R&D. The R&D process generates new ideas which add to the stock of knowledge. However, the possibilities created by new ideas do not just add up, they multiply. Hence, at the national level the returns to expenditure on R&D do not decline as the stock of knowledge expands, as do the returns to other forms of investment, such as in machinery or land, and this in turn can fuel permanent growth of national productivity.

In such an approach the long-run rate of growth is not exogenous but is determined within the economic system. Hence governments can adopt policies which can affect the long-run growth rate. Policies which stimulate investment in R&D or which improve the stock of human capital through education and training (human capital being a vital input into R&D and a crucial factor determining the effectiveness with which new ideas are applied), can influence the long-rate of growth.

In both the traditional and endogenous growth theories firms are treated as being identical. In the approach of this book the process of technological change, the generation of new ideas and the culture which determines the effectiveness of these ideas are the main determinants of the growth of productivity within firms. The continual generation of new products and processes, together with the ongoing learning process which improves the application of existing techniques, act to generate consistent growth. The extent of this growth is determined by the quality of human capital within the corporation and the corporate climate in which individual actors combine and draw upon the stock of knowledge embodied in the firm. At any point in time, the firm thus represents a collection of human and physical assets inherited from past evolution, so the growth performance of firms will differ. We will seek to show that identifying firms which have a propensity for relatively fast growth compared to other participants in the market can play an important role in assessing the effectiveness of management strategies within those firms and in helping to make informed portfolio investment decisions.

1.6 OUTLINE OF THE BOOK

In this book, after briefly reviewing the economic approach to the growth of productivity and carefully explaining our model of corporate productivity growth, we analyse the performance of a range of individual firms across a number of different sectors, but primarily chemicals, pharmaceuticals and electronics. The analysis identifies two key variables which characterise the evolution of the firm: technological performance and performance in the market. A clear prescription for a change in firm strategies can be attached to firms which perform poorly in terms of both technological advancement and selling. The model is also used to analyse the impact of firm restructuring and mergers, and as a means of assessing corporate plans for future development of an enterprise.

We also use the model to show that there is a strong positive correlation between the trend growth of a firm and its market valuation. On average, firms which are able to achieve strong growth in productivity tend to be able to generate sustained increases in profits over time, which in turn is associated with a rising stock market value. The model can be applied to identify those firms which have high trend rates of growth and which therefore offer good long-term prospects for portfolio investors. The approach can also be used to identify firms whose stock market value is inconsistent with the trend in their growth performance, such that a revaluation of the price of the stock of that company may occur.

The book continues in Chapter 2 by providing a brief non-technical review of the economic approach to economic growth. We provide more detail on the traditional model of economic growth in which technological progress is taken to be exogenous and a fuller description of the more recent endogenous growth theory, which stresses the role of research and development by firms and of human capital accumulation. We concentrate on highlighting those ideas and approaches which have influenced the development of our model of corporate growth.

Chapter 2 also provides a brief overview of the way that the firm is conceptualised in the traditional economic approach and describes an alternative view, initially propounded in the 1950s, which argues that the way firms are internally organised is important in determining performance. We therefore need to look at what happens inside firms, in terms of the way that information and ideas circulate and are processed and how decisions are made, rather than assuming, as in the traditional economic model, that decisions are made by a single rational, all-knowing entrepreneur. Most importantly, this more modern view of the firm predicts that there are always possibilities for doing things better within a firm, such that a process of continuous growth will emerge.

Chapter 3 provides a discussion of the view of the firm adopted in this book and a description of the model of corporate productivity growth. Technical details, which have previously been published in an academic business journal, are presented in Appendix 3.1, for those who wish to explore them, as is a description of the process of calibrating the model to the data for individual corporations (Appendix 3.2). These details are not necessary for progress through the rest of the book.

The model reflects two key principles, first that productivity growth is driven by technological progress and learning processes and, secondly, that the modern corporation is a complex, self-organising system. This leads to the prediction that growth is a natural process for a corporation and that such growth will tend to be sustained at a constant rate in the medium to long term. We then describe a dynamic, but simple, approach to the modelling of corporate productivity which reflects these key features. The essence of the empirical application of the model to data for actual companies is the generation of estimated growth coefficients for the evolution of productivity in each firm.

Chapter 4 is the first of the following empirical chapters that discuss the applications of the model to data for actual companies. In this chapter the emphasis is firmly upon analysing and comparing the growth performance of companies, and we seek to show how the model can be used to assess management strategies. The analysis of the trend in the growth of productivity is combined with the derivation of the growth coefficients for average wages and salaries, for employment and for the trend in operating profit per person and in total. Here we suggest a classification of firms according to whether the growth of operating profits is fuelled primarily by the growth of productivity, reflecting a strong technological performance, or by the growth of employment, reflecting a more market oriented strategy dependent upon success in marketing and selling.

Most importantly, the analysis shows how the corporation is bound by the magnitude of the trend growth rate of productivity, and this in turn can highlight corporate plans which are likely to be inconsistent or difficult to implement. The chapter also demonstrates that growth of productivity and growth of wages and salaries tend to be positively correlated. Here causality will be bi-directional. Firms where productivity, and profitability, are rising strongly will be best placed to offer rising wages and salaries. In addition, given the importance of the role of human capital and the quality of the workforce in the modern corporation, those companies which offer the best prospects for growing wages will be able to keep and attract the most able workers. This in turn will contribute to long-run productivity growth.

Chapter 5 is devoted to an analysis of mergers. The model can be applied to analyse the behaviour of the merging firms prior to the merger taking place and then use this information to project possible developments in the post-merger years. Where data are available, the model can also be used to compare pre-and post-merger performance. What matters from the perspective of the approach of this book is the nature of the corporate culture of the combined firm relative to that of the pre-merger firms. The medium-to-long-run performance of the merged firm will depend upon whether the corporate cultures of the pre-merger firms are compatible such that the growth processes of the merged firm are enhanced relative to those of the individual firms prior to the merger.

Chapter 6 provides an application of the model to investment analysis. It is shown how the information given by the model can be used to identify firms, which on the basis of past performance, and the fact that growth rates tend to be sustained, are likely to grow strongly in the future. Given the strong correlations that we observe, first between the trend rate of productivity growth and trend growth of profits and secondly between the trend rate of profit growth and the market valuation of the firm, such firms are likely to offer the best opportunities for *long-run* returns on investment. We also show how the model can demonstrate those firms which are more susceptible to cyclical swings in the economy, so that a measure of risk can be associated with the estimated trend growth coefficient and hence with the prospect for long-term return identified.

The final chapter, Chapter 7, provides some conclusions and discusses the relevance and usefulness of the model to business applications. Here we briefly discuss what our approach to the firm implies for aggregate economic behaviour in terms of national economic performance.

2 Economic Analysis of Growth: A Review

2.1 INTRODUCTION

Traditional economics has concentrated upon analysing economic growth at the aggregate or national level. The principal objective has been to explain the sustained growth of living standards in industrial countries and why the long-run rate of growth has varied across countries, particularly when the standard theory predicts that countries will tend to converge to the same long-run trend rate of growth.

The key factor generating sustained growth within the traditional or neo-classical model is *technological change*. However, technological progress in the famous Solow model is exogenous in the sense that it just appears and is not generated by the actions or decisions of economic actors in the market. Later developments of this theory provided for a public research sector to provide new technologies to the industrial sector, which itself undertook no research. In the 1990s attention focused upon how technological change might be generated within the economic system and how this affected the rate of economic growth. This 'endogenous growth theory' shows how investment in R&D (the production of new ideas) and the quality of the labour force in terms of education and training (the level of human capital) can engender consistent long-run growth of income per person.

Little concern has been given in standard economics to the growth of firms. This is because the traditional economic theory of the firm is concerned with the static allocation of resources and the conditions which generate a welfare-maximising equilibrium outcome. Thus, the firm, which is itself a vaguely defined concept, is analysed only from the point of view of understanding the problem of price determination and how the resources of an economy can be allocated in the most efficient way between alternative uses. Essentially, the traditional theory of the firm, which still dominates undergraduate microeconomic textbooks, demonstrates that under competitive market conditions firms will combine resources to produce goods and services in such a way that, given the demand of consumers, an efficient allocation

11

of a nation's resources is achieved. In other words, an alternative allocation of economic resources could not produce a greater amount of economic welfare in the country.

Within the confines of the traditional economic theory of the firm, the growth of a firm is seen simply as the increase in output of a product or products such that the firm reaches its optimum size (the level of output at which average costs are minimised) for a given technology. The theory can explain the advantages of a firm being of a particular size and sees the growth of the firm as the adjustment of size as relevant to given conditions. However, the nature of equilibrium analysis, whereby a stable outcome must be achieved, requires that growth of the firm in this sense cannot occur indefinitely. Thus, there are clear limits to the size of the firm without which a clearly determined equilibrium position could not be found. The sustained growth of multi-product firms over time, where technology is constantly changing and new products and processes are continually being introduced, is not an issue that can be assessed within, or is of relevance to, this traditional theory.

In the traditional view firms have 'no insides'[1] and there is no need to inquire or analyse what happens inside firms. However, the organisational features of firms and the way that these determine and limit the growth of the firm has received attention amongst a group of economists and business analysts away from the mainstream of mathematical economic analysis. Underlying this approach, together with that of this book, is the view that growth is a normal process which leads to a progressive evolution of the firm. The size of the enterprise, rather than being the focus of attention, becomes a 'more or less incidental result of a continuous on-going or "unfolding" process'.[2] An important feature shared by this approach to the firm and the model developed in this book is that the sustained growth of productivity and growth of profits in the long term are synonymous. In our approach, increasing productivity is necessary to generate growth of profitability, while investments in R&D which provide for future increases in productivity, have to be financed out of the profitable surplus of the firm. This chapter seeks to provide a background by which to put into perspective the model of corporate growth which is developed in Chapter 3 and then used as the basis for modelling and analysing the growth of specific corporations in subsequent chapters. We start by briefly reviewing the traditional, Solow, model of growth and then discuss recent developments regarding the role of innovation and ideas captured in endogenous growth models. We then look at the work of non-mainstream economists who have sought to understand the firm as an organisation and have analysed the factors which lead to a process of growth within the firm. This approach provides a stepping stone from the traditional economic theory of the firm to the approach of this book which sees the firm as a complex, self-organising entity, which with constant investment in R&D and continual learning processes, is able to generate sustained growth of productivity and hence profits within the firm. The approach developed in this book places emphasis on the role of technological change and the way that the corporate culture within the enterprise determines the extent to which technological opportunities are translated into rising productivity.

2.2   THE TRADITIONAL OR NEO-CLASSICAL APPROACH TO ECONOMIC GROWTH

We start by briefly describing the traditional approach to economic growth which is useful in understanding subsequent, more modern theories which stress the importance of technological change, human capital and learning processes. These are some of the key elements of the model of corporate growth which we develop in Chapter 3. However, our model is able to explain differences in growth rates between different corporations, to which standard economics gives no attention, and is based upon a quite different premise concerning the nature of the firm, which we will seek to highlight over these two chapters.

In the traditional economic approach, the firm combines labour (workers) and capital (machines and factories) to produce goods and services. The individual rational decision-makers within firms act in a way that optimal choices are always taken. In a market economy without imperfections to the market mechanism it can be shown that firms throughout the economy will utilise the limited resources of labour and capital in the most efficient way in terms of maximising the level of economic welfare.

This conclusion is predicated on a number of important assumptions about the firm and the process of production. The most important of these are that the productivity of labour declines as the number of workers using a fixed amount of capital increases and, similarly, that the productivity of capital will fall as more machines are combined with a given number of workers. The economic term for this feature is known as the 'law of diminishing marginal returns'. It implies that each additional worker employed will produce less output than the previous person hired for a given amount of machinery and business infrastructure, and that each additional unit of investment in machinery will add a smaller amount to the total of goods or services produced by the firm for a given number of employees.

If we briefly shift to the national level and assume that all firms are essentially identical, as traditional economics would suggest, then for a given technology by which labour and capital are combined there are limits to which, for a fixed population, greater output can be achieved by raising the level of investment. In other words if population growth is relatively low, as it is in most advanced industrial countries, then in the long run the incentive to invest will tend to disappear. The fact that investment has continued since the industrial revolution, with the ratio of capital to output in industry remaining relatively constant, suggests that other factors are changing so as to maintain the attractiveness of investment in high-income countries. The most obvious of these factors is technological change which raises the productivity of both capital and labour over time. In the traditional model, technological progress implies an increase in the amount of goods or services produced by a given combination of resources.

The other major assumption of relevance here is that if firms increase the number of workers and the amount of capital simultaneously and in the same proportion then the amount of output will also increase by this same proportion. This is known as the 'assumption of constant returns to scale' and it implies that if the number of workers and the amount of machinery are, say, doubled, then output will also double.

This approach to the firm and these key assumptions, which were emphasised by the pioneers of economic analysis – Adam Smith and David Ricardo – form the basis of the traditional economic approach to growth, which dominated the discipline in the 1960s, 1970s and much of the 1980s. The key originator of the neo-classical growth theory is the American economist Robert Solow.[3] He showed how, in this traditional framework, that the growth of aggregate output would be determined by the rate of growth of investment in capital, the growth of the population and a residual reflecting technological change.

The key predictions and implications of the Solow model are that:

- There can be sustained increases in output per worker only if *technology is continually improving*. In the absence of technological change the only way that output per worker can rise is through increased investment in capital. However, since there are assumed to be diminishing returns to capital (each new unit of investment generates less output than the previous unit) then there is a limit to the extent to which the accumulation of capital can lead to increases in output per worker. Hence the only way for incomes per head to rise consistently is for technological change to continually raise the amount of output that can be achieved from the combination of a given set of resources.

A drawback of the Solow model is that technological progress is exogenous to the economic system and is therefore not influenced by the actions of firms or consumers. Thus, in this model the rate of technological progress is not determined by decisions taken by firms or by governments and appears like manna from heaven. This implies that all firms have access to the same identical technology and grow at the same rate.

• Economies with *lower levels of productivity or output per worker* should grow faster than economies which have considerably higher levels of output per worker. This again follows from the assumption of diminishing returns to capital. At low levels of income the returns to each extra unit of investment, in terms of the additional output that is generated, are high relative to investment in high-income countries where the marginal return to capital will be lower. Hence, investment in capital should occur at a faster rate in low-income countries and this will generate faster growth of output per worker than in rich countries.

Thus, the theory predicts convergence of growth rates across countries. However, convergence is conditional, since the long-run level of capital per worker, and hence the long-run level of output per worker, will depend upon national characteristics such as the savings rate and the rate of population growth. More recently, a number of studies has suggested additional factors which condition the rate of convergence, such as political stability, the presence of effective laws and institutions to protect the property rights of the individual, lack of corruption, openness to trade and investment in education.

Another way of interpreting the Solow model is that the current growth rate of a country is determined by the difference between the current level of aggregate output or income and the long-run potential level of output. If a country has nearly achieved its potential level of output then the growth of income per person will tend to be low.

However, sustained growth can be achieved with technological progress, which acts continually to shift outwards the potential level of output. This idea is utilised in our approach to growth of the firm which is developed fully in Chapter 3. Here the growth of the firm is influenced by the potential level of output of the firm for a given technology. But again technological progress continually pushes outwards the potential level of output per person. However, an important feature of the model of this book is that the capacity of the firm to exploit the technological opportunities that are available is determined by the corporate culture of the enterprise.

2.3 MODERN ECONOMIC THEORIES OF GROWTH

The neo-classical approach to growth outlined above dominated economic thinking from the 1960s to the 1980s. However, the prediction that the return on investment and the rate of capital accumulation would fall as output per head increased, owing to diminishing returns to capital, was inconsistent with the observed persistence of investment rates over long periods of time. In addition, it was always recognised that treating technological progress as entirely exogenous was unsatisfactory. The main development in response to these disadvantages with the Solow model has been the introduction of knowledge and human capital.

One idea introduced by Kenneth Arrow[4] is that knowledge might accumulate through learning by doing. Arrow specified the state of knowledge as being determined by the cumulative amount of investment in machinery and other capital equipment that had previously been made in the economy as a whole. This knowledge then contributes to improvements in the productivity of the other resources that are utilised in the industrial sector. Specifically, the productivity of labour is enhanced as experience in investment is accumulated over time. The consistent improvement in knowledge that comes from accumulated investment ensures that investment in capital goods remains profitable even at higher levels of output and so provides a basis for sustained growth of output per person. However, it is important to note that in Arrow's model this type of technical progress arises as an accidental consequence of the normal decisions of firms to invest in capital goods.

We adopt the essence of the idea of learning by doing in the model we develop in this book, but specify that it is the amount of learning and experience *within* the firm that matters. Within the modern corporation, the productivity of labour is an increasing function of the level of experience within the firm, as reflected by the accumulated level of output. The presence of a learning curve has been highlighted by studies of firm-level behaviour, most notably by the Boston Consulting Group (BCG) in the 1970s. In the model of this book, the way in which this pool of knowledge within the firm is drawn upon is determined by the corporate culture within the enterprise, which varies from firm to firm. We return to discuss this issue of learning processes within the firm in much more detail in Chapter 3.

These notions concerning knowledge and the role of experience have been extended in models which explicitly recognise the incentive for firms to invest in R&D to generate new ideas which improve existing techniques and generate new products and new production processes. At the forefront of these developments has been the work of Paul Romer, who is most closely associated with the introduction of theories of 'endogenous growth'. Romer[5] treats knowledge as being created by conscious decisions by firms to invest in R&D activities. Firms invest in knowledge which they combine with other resources to produce goods and services and also to produce additional knowledge. Growth is generated by investment in physical capital which is in turn driven by the results of investment in R&D. Technological innovations tend to raise the return to capital and so make attractive continuing investments in machinery and other equipment. However, some of the knowledge created within the firm spills over to other firms, so that in making their own decisions to invest in generating new knowledge firms inadvertently add to the stock of publicly available knowledge.

A key element of this approach is that the returns to investment in knowledge creation do not decline in the long run. The acquisition of knowledge leads to increments in the productivity of labour. However, the incentive to invest in knowledge generation does not diminish as output per head increases and hence the profitability of investing in machinery and equipment remains positive. Technical progress again ensures that investment is sustained over long periods. However, in this case technical progress is endogenously determined by the intentional decisions of firms to direct resources, through investment, to the generation of additional knowledge.

One reason why diminishing returns to investment in R&D do not set in is that the impact of investment in new ideas is determined by the existing stock of knowledge. Thus, new ideas interact with existing knowledge. The possibilities that are generated by new ideas do not expand additively, but multiplicatively.[6] In addition, knowledge has the property, not possessed by the other factors of production – physical capital and labour – that its use is not restricted to one particular application. This is likely to be important in large complex multi-product corporations where a new idea can have a wide range of applications within the enterprise.

Again, the key elements of this approach are present in the model of corporate growth which we develop in Chapter 3. In addition to the benefits that accumulated production experience has on labour productivity, firms invest in R&D activities to generate ideas and solutions which add to the long-run potential output of the individual workers within the corporation. The impact on productivity growth being determined by the research base within the firm as reflected by cumulated investment in R&D. In contrast to the economic approaches to growth discussed here the approach developed in this book places greater emphasis on internal factors within the firm which determine the culture within the enterprise in which new ideas can be communicated and the solutions to perceived problems implemented. This corporate culture dictates the extent to which investment in R&D and accumulated production experience is translated into sustained increments in productivity within the firm.

Another important line of development in economic growth theory has been attention to the role of human capital. In many ways this is complementary to the work which has endogenised technical progress through the decisions of firms to invest in R&D. Indeed, the distinction between 'human capital' and 'knowledge' is not always apparent. It is clear that in the models discussed above highly skilled and educated workers are likely to play an important role in R&D and the generation of ideas, but the role of human capital in influencing growth is indirect. It is investment in R&D which is the primary stimulus to sustained long-run growth. However, other studies have sought to explicitly represent the role of human capital in economic development and growth.

A straightforward definition of human capital is 'a set of specialised skills that agents can acquire by devoting time to an activity called "schooling." The more time that an individual spends in school, the greater is the measure of human capital that the individual acquires.'[7] However, in the approach to the firm developed in this book human capital is more broadly defined to capture the improvements in the productivity of the individual that derive from accumulated experience and learning processes. This is more in tune with the definitions of Theodore Schultz and Gary Becker that human capital captures all of the capacities of the individual likely to contribute to his or her productive effectiveness.[8] More generally, human capital differs from other forms of capital in that it cannot be separated from the person. An individual cannot be divorced from their knowledge, skills and motivation in the way that financial and physical capital assets can be moved and used regardless of the location of their owner.

The principal approach has been to extend the basic Solow model by including human capital as an additional factor which is necessary for the production of goods and services in the modern economy. Educated and well-trained people will tend to use capital, in terms of machines and equipment, more effectively, thus raising the productivity of capital. The skills of the workforce also play an important role in the way that new technologies and ideas are applied in practice within the firm. In addition, such people tend to spread the benefits of their education and experience to other workers, who learn from them and in turn become more productive. Hence, increasing levels of skill, education and experience tend to raise the productivity of all factors involved in the production process. Again, this provides a means by which the return on investment in physical capital goods may not fall in the long run, so that investment will continue even as capital is accumulated allowing sustained growth of productivity.

To summarise, the traditional economic approach to growth stresses the role of capital accumulation in generating rising incomes. However, the theory suggests that growth will tend to decline the more that capital is accumulated since the return to capital and the incentive to invest fall the more capital that is applied to a given amount of labour. In the long run, if populations are growing very slowly, then growth can be sustained only by exogenously determined improvements in technology which improve the productivity of all factors of production and so maintain the incentive to invest in capital equipment, even with high levels of accumulated capital.

Recently, economists have sought to overcome the unsatisfactory nature of treating technical progress as exogenous in the traditional model. The key feature of modern growth theory is that technical progress arises from *conscious decisions by individuals to invest in R&D* to generate new ideas or *in training and education* to improve human capital capabilities. Under these approaches the return to capital does not decline at higher levels of development since new techniques and technologies and greater efficiency from education tend to raise the productivity of all factors. In the model developed in Chapter 3, the human capital of the firm is reflected by the way in which new techniques and technologies are applied and the way in which individual workers draw upon the accumulated experience within the firm to augment their productivity. This level of human capital interacts with the corporate culture of the firm to determine the effectiveness with which the possibilities for new techniques are communicated throughout the firm, the way in which possible technical solutions to identified problems are developed and the efficiency with which these new ideas are implemented.

This emphasis on the way that relationships are organised within the firm is commensurate with some recent literature on growth from a sociological perspective which stresses the importance of civic and societal values in affecting the growth performance of communities.[9] This literature suggests that the way in which individuals cooperate and interact with each other, on the basis of obligations and trust, plays an important role in explaining contemporary economic performance. As such the model of this book places at the forefront of explanations of differential growth performance across firms the nature of internal processes within the firm. Both traditional and more modern growth theories pay little or no attention to what happens within firms. However, this issue has been carefully assessed by a particular strand of economics which, unlike the traditional theory, has sought to explain the growth of firms, rather than trying to explain the key facts which characterise the growth of countries.

2.4   APPROACHES TO CORPORATE GROWTH

Firms are among the basic elements of a market economy. However, the growth process of individual firms receives little or no attention in the standard economic approaches that have been outlined above. In many ways the theory of the firm in economics has remained distinct from the theory of economic growth. The theory of the firm concentrates upon explaining the advantages of a particular size of firm, given external conditions. Firm growth is seen as the movement from one optimum size to another as conditions change. There is no coherent attempt to explain the growth of firms as a continuous process, and this economic theory cannot explain why growth rates may vary between firms in a particular sector. No attention is given to what happens inside firms and whether there are any internal constraints upon their growth. In these approaches the factors constraining growth are exogenous to, or outside of the control of, the firm.

In the 1950s and 1960s alternative approaches to the treatment of firms in economics were developed which rejected the notion of an optimum size of the firm and stressed that it is in the nature of modern corporate firms to grow continuously. One of the principal contributions to this literature came from Edith Penrose[10] who highlighted the importance of the managerial and administrative processes which take place within firms and who viewed the firm as an economic institution. She suggested that 'as management tries to make the best use of the resources available, a truly "dynamic" interacting process occurs which encourages continuous growth but limits the rate of growth'. We proceed to give a more detailed review of Penrose's ideas which take us away from the traditional neo-classical view of the firm which dominates economic approaches and moves us some way toward the context in which firms are modelled in this study as complex, evolving, self-organising structures.

The starting point for Penrose's work is the view that the traditional economic theory of the firm is inadequate and inappropriate for an analysis of the growth of firms. This reflects in part that the principal concern of microeconomic theory is not the growth of firms but the issue of how resources are allocated and role of prices and markets in this process. A firm is typically regarded as an individual decision-taker whose role is to combine factors of production in technological processes to produce goods or services. This view of the firm provides for an analysis which demonstrates that a system of interrelated goods and factor markets dominated by individual decision-makers will generate an equilibrium allocation of resources. Further, it shows that under competitive market conditions this allocation will be the most efficient out of the many alternative possible allocations of resources[11].

The focus on equilibrium outcomes in the standard economic approach requires that there be limits to the expansion of output by the individual firm. Without a constraint upon the size of the firm a determinate static equilibrium outcome cannot be found. This constraint upon the size of the firm comes either from the assumption that the average cost of producing a given product will rise after a certain level of output is achieved or that the revenue gained from additional sales will eventually fall owing to the limitation of the market. However, in practice firms are continually upgrading the technologies that they apply and are constantly introducing new products so that the technological and market constraints upon the size of firms are consistently evaded.

This traditional economic approach clearly abstracts from the actual complex organisational structure of firms. This is appropriate if the way that firms are organised has little bearing on the resource allocation process, which is the focus of the economic analysis. This is a contentious assumption. It is increasingly difficult to accept that the modern-day corporation behaves in a way analogous to a firm where decisions are made by a single rational individual.

In modern corporations, decisions tend to be taken jointly and on the basis of collaboration between a group of individuals. The environment in which this collaboration takes place, the way that ideas are communicated and acted upon within the firm – the corporate culture of the firm – is an important determinant of the long-run development of the organisation. We will return to this issue in more detail in Chapter 3. What needs to be explained is the dynamic evolution of modern multi-product corporations, which are complex institutions, continually innovating and accumulating experience, leading to the consistent introduction of new products and more efficient processes.

In the work of Penrose and others, the firm is viewed as an administrative organisation which acts to make use of the productive resources available to it to produce goods and services. It is assumed that resources are used according to plans which are developed and implemented within the firm. The resources of the firm include its tangible physical assets, such as plant, equipment and land, as well as human resources. Firms are assumed to make investment decisions on the basis of increasing profits in the long run. In addition, it is assumed that profits are sought primarily to provide for future investment – that is, profits are a necessary condition for growth. In this way 'growth and profits become equivalent as the criteria for the selection of investment programmes'.[12]

For such firms there are always possibilities for growth arising from the opportunity to use existing resources more efficiently. It is argued that a pool of unutilised productive resources will always be found within a firm so that there will be inducements for it to use them more effectively and so to grow. However, as the firm expands to make more effective use of existing resources it will require the acquisition of additional resources, the underutilisation of which will in turn offer incentives for further expansion. In other words there is a continual process of expansion due to ever-present opportunities to use existing productive resources more effectively. Thus the growth of firms is a process in which the productive possibilities of the firm are consistently being pushed outwards as the firm strives to make the most efficient use of the resources available to it.

2.5 CONCLUSIONS

This chapter has attempted to provide a brief non-technical overview of the key elements of traditional and more modern economic theories of growth and highlight which concepts are of relevance to the model of corporate growth which is developed in Chapter 3.

The clear messages from economic theory are that growth is primarily a result of investment in physical capital goods and technological change. The latter is crucial since in its absence growth will eventually dry up owing to diminishing returns to capital, a feature inconsistent with the evolution of modern industrial economies over the past 150 years. Technological progress, learning by doing and improvements in human capital act to raise the productivity of factors of production and so push back the onset of diminishing returns, thereby maintaining the incentive to invest and the basis for persistent growth.

Recent developments in economic theory have shown how technological progress can result from the conscious decisions of firms and individuals to invest in R&D and in extending the stock of human capital. In this way economic growth becomes endogenous and there develop mechanisms which ensure consistent growth over time.

The economic approach seeks to explain the growth of countries but is barren in explaining the growth of firms. In particular, it is unable to explain why some firms grow faster than others even within the same sector. Underlying the traditional economic approach is an abstract view of firms as single decision-makers so that no attention needs to be given to organisational processes within the firm. The approach of Penrose, on the other hand, demonstrates that the resources of a firm have to be *organised*. Organisational structures and processes and managerial abilities are thus crucial elements in explanations of how firms evolve over time.

These essential ingredients to an understanding of corporate growth appear in the model developed in Chapter 3. Technological progress and learning processes offer firms the opportunities for sustained growth. However, the rate of growth is determined by the way in which the firm is able to draw upon the experience it possesses in its constituent parts, the culture that dictates the way that individuals interact within the firm and the way that information is processed and acted upon. The view which underlies our model of the firm is a modern one of a complex but evolving institution. A key feature of the subsequent work in the book is empirical application of the model to data for a range of corporations which allows for a comparative perspective on firm performance and provides for an analysis of the link between the trend in performance and stock market valuation.

3 Modelling the Growth of Corporate Productivity

3.1 INTRODUCTION

In this chapter we present our model of corporate growth which is based upon strong theoretical reasoning but is also designed to be applicable empirically and in particular to be of use in explaining the different growth performance of various corporations. Here we provide the underlying basis of the model in an intuitive manner without the use of technical and particularly mathematical terms. A technical specification of the model is provided in Appendix 3.1 (p.39), while a discussion of how the model can be calibrated to available data for specific corporations is provided in Appendix 3.2 (p.46). The basic objective of the model is to explain why corporations tend to exhibit persistent growth of labour productivity over time and why growth rates differ between corporations competing in similar markets. There are two key elements to the model which are first discussed in the chapter: first, the nature of the firm and then, secondly, technological progress and learning processes. In the final part of the chapter we bring these concepts together to provide a full discussion of the model of the growth of productivity within modern corporations.

In Chapter 2 we discussed how technological progress has played a major role in economic models of national growth of productivity. Initially, in the Solow model technological innovation was treated as taking place outside the economy with technical progress occurring in a purely random manner. This is appropriate if scientific discovery is the main force behind technical progress and such discoveries are made by scientists working in laboratories which are quite separate from the industrial sector. Recent economic theories have sought to model technical progress as being the result of conscious decisions to invest in R&D made within the industrial sector. In this model innovation takes place within the firm as a direct result of resources being devoted to R&D activities. In this way, technical progress is, as Schumpeter first suggested, an integral part of a market economy. Capitalist enterprise is the 'propelling force' behind technical advancement.[1]

Despite popular notions, in many sectors it is not major inventions which drive technological advancement. Rather, it is numerous and continuous improvements to products and processes together with the increments to productivity that arise from accumulated learning within an enterprise. This requires effective communication between all elements of the enterprise so that the possibilities for such improvements and the impact of the chosen solutions are known. Hence, the corporate culture within an enterprise, which dictates the way that individuals within the corporation interact and the way that information flows are acted upon, becomes a crucial determinant of the way in which new technical opportunities are translated into the growth of productivity within the firm.

Here, we start by discussing the nature of the firm and the way that individuals behave within firms. The model developed here is derived from quite different premises from those underlying the traditional economic approach to the firm. We are not concerned with analysing stable equilibrium outcomes which are not relevant to the study of the *process* of growth. We concentrate upon the firm as being a complex dynamic organisation which is far from equilibrium. Complexity follows from the interactions which take place between individuals within the corporation and from the links between the different components of the multi-levelled structures which modern corporations exhibit. In this framework the individuals face difficult problems but do not have unlimited cognitive abilities to solve them deductively. The rationality of the individual is bounded so that learning and experience play an important role in the way that the individuals order and respond to the problems that they confront.

The more modern view of the firm adopted here is one in which the presence of increasing returns generates path-dependence, so that history matters, and a range of outcomes for the firm are possible. Again, this is in contrast to the traditional economic approach where the nature of diminishing returns helps to ensure stable and predictable equilibrium outcomes. Borrowing ideas from the physical sciences, which have subsequently been applied to the analysis of social systems, we argue that even in an unstable and unpredictable environment organisations are constantly changing their form and structure, and as a result of this they thrive. Organisations which are pushed away from stable situations tend to experiment and innovate to find new ways of proceeding. They *self-organise* to bring some order out of the chaotic and unstable environment that they inhabit. Even in this dynamic world there are limits on the range of behaviour, so that it is possible for regular patterns to emerge. In the context of this book this takes the form of the consistent and sustained growth of productivity for modern corporations. It is to these issues regarding the nature of the firm and the way that the individual is comprehended that we now turn.

3.2   THE COMPLEX SELF-ORGANISING ENTERPRISE

As we noted in Chapter 2, conventional economics has paid little attention to what happens inside firms, in the way that decisions are made, the environment in which individuals interact and the structure in which information is communicated throughout the enterprise. The model of corporate growth developed here is based on the premise that these are crucial issues in the modern industrial corporation. The modern corporate enterprise is seen as a complex organisation which is continually evolving. This contrasts with the classical economic assumption that, under the influence of diminishing returns, an economic process will always tend towards a stable equilibrium or steady-state solution. In this section we describe in more detail the notions of complexity and self-organisation which underlie an evolutionary system which tends to generate increasing returns. The presence of increasing returns implies that there will not be a unique equilibrium outcome and that growth may become a self-reinforcing process. We start by briefly discussing the basic assumptions concerning individual behaviour.

3.2.1   The cognitive abilities of the individual

In the traditional economic approach the decision of the firm of what to produce and how is determined by a single rational entrepreneur. Homo Economicus[2] applies rational, deductive reasoning – deriving a conclusion from applying perfect logical processes based upon well-defined premises – to solve the economic problems that he or she faces.[3] In short, economic agents are intelligent, perhaps super-intelligent, and they maximise. The latter implies that the individual will always choose the best of the available alternatives. As a result when individuals interact the system will tend towards a stable equilibrium where each individual is doing the best that they can given what other individuals are doing. This mathematical approach, which began to dominate in the 1940s following the work of John Hicks and Paul Samuelson, was quite different from the ways that earlier economists treated the individual. In the first half of the twentieth century economists such as Irving Fisher and John Maynard Keynes considered psychological factors in their explanations of economic behaviour. As such, economics in the early part of the twentieth century was much more of a social science.[4]

As many authors have pointed out the standard economic approach requires a lot of the cognitive ability of the individual, much more than they can reasonably be expected to deliver.[5] An alternative view is that the cognitive abilities of the individual are limited so that beyond a certain degree of complication or difficulty logical processes cease to cope. In this case, the rationality of the individual is bounded. For most of the modern problems that the economic individual faces the issue is thus not one of thinking logically to produce a rational and consistent course of action but one of trying to structure and make sense of the situations that they encounter. *Learning and feedback from the environment* play a crucial role in helping the individual to interpret the problems that they face. In this way experience leads to actions being derived by a process of inductive reasoning, which is in turn complicated by the need to take account of the actions of others which are always changing. So under this approach individuals exist in a world of high complexity and deal with the problems that they face on the basis of learning and adaptation. Knowledge, based upon observation, is used in combination with deduction to make decisions and to determine actions. Further, the process of learning occurs in the networks of social interactions within which the individual is bound within the firm. Individuals learn from each other and this process will be dictated by the nature of the social networks in the firm.

This is not to imply that the typical economic approach of maximising individuals and equilibrium outcomes is of no use. There is a range of issues where this static textbook model of behaviour helps to understand specific issues. This model is of use when it helps to organise and simplify the understanding of particular economic issues without taking us too far away from realistic assumptions about behaviour. However, we argue here that this approach has little relevance to trying to understand the dynamic process by which modern multi-product corporations evolve and grow over time. In this context it is not feasible to concentrate upon equilibrium solutions. Further, we think that the way that individuals interact *within* the firm is important in influencing the direction that the firm takes and ultimately influences the success with which the firm is able to grow. This interaction often leads to a process whereby decisions are made jointly through *collaboration*. The way that this collaboration takes place is partly a reflection of the corporate culture that is established within the firm.

3.2.2 The firm as a complex, self-organising system

The firm today comprises a group of individuals and provides a structure, or institutional framework, which often has many different levels, in which those individuals interact. This leads to the view of the modern corporation as a complex social organisation. An understanding of complexity, we believe, is necessary to understand how modern corporate organisations behave. 'Complexity' may be formally defined as the intricate relationships that characterise the interaction of agents, which adapt and evolve in a changing environment. Complexity therefore arises from 'the inter-twining or inter-connectivity of elements within a system and between a system and its environment'.[6] In social systems, such as firms, connectivity arises since decisions and actions by any one element or individual will affect all the other elements or individuals which are related within the system. The precise nature of this effect will depend upon the 'state' of the individual and of the system. This in turn is determined by its history as well as its structure. Complexity arising from connectivity is not just limited to interactions between individuals within the firm but also to the way that individuals interact with information technology (IT) and with systems of ideas.

Much of the analysis of complex systems has been undertaken in the physical sciences, primarily following the work of Nobel Prize winner Ilya Prigogine[7] at the *Université Libre de Bruxelles*, and subsequently at the Santa Fe Institute in the USA.[8] More recently, researchers have been looking at the application of the initial ideas of complexity to social systems and organisations.

Prigogine shifted the emphasis of analysis in the physical sciences away from static equilibrium towards non-equilibrium situations. This has led to a number of key conclusions, notably:

- That *non-equilibrium may be a source of organisation* – that is, that self-organisation may be an important feature of complex systems. Systems far from equilibrium survive and thrive since they are forced to create new patterns of relationships and different structures. With regard to social systems, such as firms, this implies that when the organisation is pushed away from established patterns of behaviour then individuals will experiment and find new patterns of relationships, different structures and alternative ways of working.

This is quite different from the underlying fundamental principles of physics and economics that bodies and organisations will always tend towards an equilibrium solution. Experience suggests otherwise. Hence attention needs to be focused upon process just as much as upon outcome. So, firms are involved in a continual dynamic process of growth and evolution far from static equilibrium. What we seek to describe below is the mechanism by which the firm changes through time.

- Since organisations which are far from equilibrium tend to experiment and explore they will be characterised by the *continual generation of new possibilities and new potentials*. This entails that improvements are always possible[9] and will be implemented regularly. Successful firms are incessantly re-specifying themselves in terms of how they operate and the products that they produce.
- That organisations which are far from equilibrium are characterised by *irreversible processes*. In conventional economics there are negative feedback effects or diminishing returns which ensure that a stable and predictable equilibrium outcome will be achieved. Negative feedback implies that at equilibrium any large changes or shocks are offset by reactions that they generate.[10]
- However, in practice it is clear that increasing returns are embodied in a range of economic processes. We argued in Chapter 2 that the production of ideas, which are fundamental to economic growth, is unlikely to be subject to decreasing returns. Increasing returns lead to positive feedback effects and irreversible processes. Hence, small changes can become magnified and a process of *self-reinforcing growth* can be instigated. The presence of increasing returns leads to the property of path-dependence whereby current evolution is locked in to previous events. In this way history matters.
- Since the stabilising forces of diminishing returns cannot be relied upon, the state of the economic system, or of the organisation, becomes unpredictable and unstable, with many possible outcomes. Small changes in conditions can result in major adjustments in the behaviour of the system. In addition, complex systems regularly face points of bifurcation or crossroads where the direction of the system can change. For example, the firm is constantly faced with *decisional crossroads*, concerning the development of new products

or application of new technologies; the choices taken determine the direction that the firm will take.

However, a principal feature of self-organising systems is that they generate order out of chaos. There are limits to the range of possible behaviour and so there are constraints on the degree of instability. Complex systems can perform in regular, predictable ways under certain conditions, but under other conditions exhibit unstable behaviour. Firms, which are dynamic, constantly changing systems can change in a regular manner. This is what we argue below in regard to the growth of corporate productivity in the long term. When the productivity gains from a particular technique or technology are close to being exhausted, the firm is faced with the decision of which of a range of new techniques and technologies to implement. The precise choice that will be taken cannot be unambiguously predicted beforehand but nevertheless, under certain conditions, the choices that are taken at regular intervals will lead to consistent and sustained growth of productivity.

- *In complex organisations structure matters.* Network-based structures define and regulate the way that individuals interact. In addition, the complexity of modern firms arises, in part, because they are multi-layered organisations. The resulting structure need not necessarily be hierarchical in that some lower-level components may be part of a number of higher-level entities and there may be interactions between entities at many different levels of the organisation. Actions and decisions taken by components at any one level of the organisation are therefore constrained and influenced by other components both at that level and at different levels within the firm.

  In our modelling approach this structure reflects the corporate culture of the enterprise which determines how interactions within the firm are organised and governed. What is important in a dynamic, innovating system is how information and ideas are communicated throughout the organisation and how this information is acted upon. In other words the culture within the organisation determines the effectiveness by which experience and new ideas are translated into actual outcomes, namely into rising productivity within the firm.

So self-organisation is a crucial feature of modern corporate enterprises. In general terms, self-organisation is the spontaneous ordering of the elements of a system into coherent new structures or patterns. For example, individual organisms, such as termites, establish societies of organisms which interact with other societies and the environment to produce an ecosystem. People interact with one another to establish firms and markets to satisfy their material needs.

Given this view of the firm we are able to concentrate on its dynamic growth process, which may be far from a static equilibrium, the focus of the traditional neo-classical approach to the firm. But just as the neo-classical economic model seeks to provide a simple description of the static resource allocation problem, the model developed here is also a simplified view of the process of growth, the simplicity entering through the straightforward dynamics that underlie the system. In particular, the model revolves around a simple process whereby technical progress generates sustained growth at a constant rate (exponential growth) over a substantial period. We will seek to demonstrate that this simple approach is in fact a reasonable representation of the growth processes that modern corporations exhibit. First we turn to a more detailed discussion of technical progress.

3.3 TECHNICAL PROGRESS

In the model developed here technological advancement plays a crucial role in the sustained growth of the enterprise by providing for continual improvements in the productive potential of each individual in the production unit. Technological change is incorporated through two key mechanisms: the *experience effect* and the *innovation effect*. The experience effect allows for the potential productivity of each worker to rise as accumulated production experience increases. The innovation effect shows how expenditure on research and development raises potential productivity. The relative strength of the experience and the innovation effects will depend upon the characteristics of the industry and the nature of the firm. The combination of these two effects leads to a constant trend in technological progress on which the firm is able to draw. However, the extent to which greater experience and innovation are translated into higher productivity depends upon the corporate culture within each enterprise. We now discuss the experience and the innovation effect in turn.

3.3.1 Experience and learning

We noted in Chapter 2 that learning processes have been identified as being important elements in the process of economic growth and in explaining the attainment of sustained increases in productivity. Here we believe that learning processes and experience in general play a crucial role in the evolution of the firm. This view is supported by extensive and well-documented evidence from firms, the principal source being studies in the 1960s and 1970s by the Boston Consulting Group (BCG).[11] The BCG observed for a number of industries that costs tended to decline as experience, as measured by accumulated output, increased. Here 'experience' includes not only learning processes but also gains from specialisation within the firm as the magnitude of total output rises. As a general conclusion the Group concluded that the 'costs of value added decline approximately 20 to 30 per cent in real terms each time accumulated experience is doubled'. In other words value added per head or productivity tended to rise with experience.

The BCG also made clear that these benefits from experience within the firm were not automatic and that their attainment depended crucially on the competence of management to ensure that available opportunities for raising productivity were fully exploited as output expands. Here we go further and hypothesise that the experience effect depends upon the way in which individual workers are able to draw upon the accumulated experience of all of the agents working within the firm. The impact of experience on productivity will depend upon motivation, education, training and the corporate culture or environment which dictates the nature of interactions between individual agents within the firm. These factors will differ between firms, so that the impact of a given increase in experience on productivity will vary across corporations even within the same sector. The experience effect instils a natural tendency towards growth and expansion for those firms which are already producing in an industry. Thus, the experience effect is an important element in explaining the persistent growth of many of the large corporations that we observe today. However, in the long run, this effect in isolation would lead to monopolies dominating all industries. Monopolies are prevented or undermined, however, by technological change which generates new products and processes to counter the tendency toward monopoly. We now turn to discuss the issue of innovation and technological change.

3.3.2 Innovation

The notion that technological progress is primarily driven by random scientific discoveries has increasingly been questioned. In 1966

Schmookler[12] reported the results of a study of almost 1000 inventions in the petroleum refining, paper production, railway and farming industries, and concluded that there were no cases in which scientific discovery provided the stimulus to subsequent inventions. Instead, the primary stimulus was 'the recognition of a costly problem to be solved or a potentially profitable opportunity to be seized; in short, a technical problem or opportunity evaluated in economic terms'.[13]

This is the situation we envisage within firms. Opportunities for the development of new processes and techniques, which can be applied to improve the production of a particular product, and the scope for product upgrading and new products continually become apparent. The firm provides an environment in which there is always a need for, and potential benefits from, new ideas. As in Romer's national models, these new ideas interact with the existing stock of knowledge within the firm to generate a multiplicity of possible applications throughout the whole of the corporation. Just as at the national level, there is no reason to believe that the returns within the firm to additional expenditures on innovation will diminish the more that that the stock of knowledge within the firm expands. This again provides a mechanism whereby additional investments in capital goods remain profitable and are not subject to diminishing returns.

Another important concept is that ideas and information are not only an output of R&D but are also a crucial input to inventive activity. This entails that it is not only current expenditures on R&D that generate new products and processes within the firm but rather accumulated expenditures. In addition, it is suggested that innovation can be a self-perpetuating process in the sense that expenditures on R&D generate new ideas which then facilitate the generation of further knowledge. Thus, knowledge generation will not be subject to any limits, which again provides grounds for a sustained increase in productivity within the firm.

So away from any concept of equilibrium, firms have to innovate and apply new ideas to be able to survive. This is a feature of complex self-organising systems. The scope for, and impact of, innovation will depend upon the way that information is communicated and acted upon throughout the organisation. This follows from the observation that the main force behind innovation is the awareness of technical problems and opportunities. Hence, the abilities of the individuals within the firm, their motivation, the way that they interact – in short, the corporate culture – will all determine the effectiveness of resources devoted to innovation. This is a feature which is reflected in the model of corporate productivity which we now explain in detail.

3.4   THE MODEL OF THE GROWTH OF CORPORATE PRODUCTIVITY

Given the preceding discussion on the way that the individual determines actions and the nature of the firm as a complex evolving institution, we now move on to a more precise description of the model of corporate growth that we apply to real data for different firms in Chapter 4. Here we concentrate upon a verbal and non-technical discussion of the key elements of the model. A more technical, but not overly taxing, description of the model and the process of calibration to data are presented in Appendix 3.1 and 3.2.

We develop and apply a model of the evolution over time of corporate growth. We model the growth of corporate productivity and are not interested, *per se*, in the way that the size of the firm changes, although the change in the total number of employees is an important variable in the analysis. We will argue, and show, that just as at the national level where growth of productivity is associated with rising living standards, at the level of the corporation, rising productivity is closely correlated with increases in wages and also profits. In turn we will demonstrate in Chapter 6 the general association between the trend rate of growth of profits of the firm and the stock market valuation of that company.

Corporate productivity is measured as the average value added per employee of the corporation, value added being the difference between the value of production as it leaves the firm and the costs of externally provided inputs used by the firm to create that output. It is worth noting that most studies of corporations undertaken by business analysts concentrate upon the value of sales per employee as a measure of firm performance. Indeed this measure is often presented in company reports. The disadvantage of this is that a sustained increase in the price of an input, such as oil, which is passed on to consumers in terms of higher prices for the final product, would appear as an improvement in firm performance. The use of value added per head, on the other hand, provides a direct measure of the value that is being generated inside the firm. In this way *value added per employee* is a more generic measure of firm performance.

We now proceed to list the key elements of the model:

- At the heart of the model is the evolution of the *productive capacity of the average employee of the firm*, defined in terms of value added. This productive capacity is the amount of value added per worker which would be generated if the firm were able to fully utilise all of its assets. In practice the actual (annual) amount of value added per person is determined by the rate at which demand and cyclical conditions permit this productive capacity to be utilised.
- Productive capacity grows over time in response to investment by the firm in physical capital assets, the amount of investment being determined by the difference between the actual level of capacity utilisation and the level of capacity at which the firm just breaks even. In other words, any revenues arising from the individual's participation in the production structure which exceed the level necessary for the firm to break even, including some allowance for dividends to shareholders, are assumed to be reinvested to *increase the productive capacity of the individual in the future*.
- Technological progress, in terms of experience effects and innovation, enters the model by reducing the level of capacity utilisation at which the firm breaks even. More precisely, we take the break-even level of capacity to be determined by the ratio of current productive capacity to the maximum level of value added per worker that could be achieved with the current, given technology. Improvements in technology and techniques lead to a continual shifting outwards of this maximum feasible level of productivity and a tendency for the break-even level of productivity to decline relative to the actual level of productive capacity. This in turn entails that resources are constantly devoted to investment in physical assets, which allows for increases in productive capacity.

Here the approach adopted is analogous to the Solow model of aggregate economic growth discussed in Chapter 2. The growth rate of the firm is influenced by the gap between the current level of productive capacity per person and the maximum potential level of productivity for a given technology and fixed degree of learning. Thus, other things being equal, as the actual level of productivity of the firm approaches this potential level of value added per person, growth will tend to decline. However, this will not happen in practice since investment in R&D and the associated introduction of new techniques and products together with the impact of accumulated learning will act to *continually raise the potential level of productivity.*

- We assume that the impact upon value added per worker of the exploitation of a given technology or technique will tend to follow an S-shaped pattern. Initially, the new way of working or new technology will lead to a relatively modest increase in productivity. However, after a period of adaptation a mature phase of stronger consistent growth of productivity follows. Finally, after a further period the technology or technique becomes fully exploited and the *growth* of productivity tends to slow down. As the firm approaches this point it must decide among a range of additional and new techniques or technologies. This is the *bifurcation point.* However, as the firm continually implements new techniques and technologies having S-shaped patterns of exploitation a process of *continuous, exponential growth* will be generated. New techniques, processes and products will be introduced before the end of the mature phase of the previous technology or product.

- Hence technological innovation and learning processes lead to exponential growth in the feasible production capacity but the magnitude of the growth rate is determined by a parameter reflecting the corporate culture of the enterprise. In other words, the more conducive the corporate culture to the development and application of new techniques and products and the more effectively the benefits of experience are exploited enhances the precise impact of technological change on the growth of productivity. Other things being equal, firms with a *corporate culture favourable to the communication of ideas and the implementation of solutions to identified technical problems will tend to grow at a faster rate.*

So, a key feature of the model is the prediction of a constant rate of growth of productive capacity of the individual. In the empirical analysis to be discussed in the following chapters, the model is applied to data for individual companies, and a value for the long-run trend evolution of value added per person generated. The value of this growth coefficient will differ among companies reflecting variations in the resources devoted to R&D activities and differences in corporate culture which determine the effectiveness of such research and of learning processes. An important contribution of the model, and its underlying basis, for management is the demonstration of the constraint which is implied by the long-run growth coefficient of productivity. This will be discussed further in Chapter 4.

While the model predicts the long-run trend in productivity, actual productivity in any one year will vary according to demand conditions and changes in prices. In the main we are not concerned with these short-run movements in productivity, being primarily interested in the long-run trend about which they are dispersed. In general (as we discuss in more detail in Appendix 3.1), differences between observed values of value added per person and the trend value produced by the model strongly reflect the cyclical changes faced by firms in their particular market. However, a common trend in capacity utilisation is apparent among firms competing in the same market. Differential movements in price do not appear to be generally important. Thus, we conclude that our model captures the essential elements of the growth process with the residuals between the level of productivity predicted by the model and the actual level of productivity being determined by short-term cyclical movements.

The model also predicts the trend evolution of demand for the products of the firm. When this is combined with the predicted evolution of productivity a value for the number of employees in the firm is produced. An exercise in also undertaken to model the evolution of wages and salaries over time. By definition, the growth of operating profit will be determined by the difference between the growth of average value added per head and the growth of wages and salaries per person. This then leads to a number of issues whereby the model can be of use to management planning. For example, the model can demonstrate the employment implications of the trend in productivity growth given a continuation of the past development in wages and salaries. The implications for the growth of overall operating profits can then be derived from the predicted evolution of profits per head and the trend in the number of employees. Again, the application of the model for this type of analysis will be discussed in more detail in subsequent Chapter 4.

3.5 CONCLUSIONS

The model of the firm developed in this book is based upon a modern view of the corporation as an institution comprising a group of individuals, together with the networks which determine how those individuals interact. Decisions within the firm are not made by a single all-knowing individual, as in classical economics, but are usually made as a result of collaboration between individuals and based on the imperfect flow of information and ideas within the firm. The individuals within the firm are unable to act in the perfectly rational manner postulated in standard economics, but rather have to organise the problems that they face and respond in a way based upon experience and learning.

The firm is a complex self-organising institution far from equilibrium. This implies that the firm has to evolve to survive and, as part of this, processes are generated which lead to increasing returns and the sustained growth of productivity. The precise rate of growth of productivity is determined by the way in which the firm responds to the opportunities for improvement that are presented by expenditures on R&D and which flow from accumulated learning and experience. Firms with a strong corporate culture will tend to make the best use of new ideas and most efficiently identify and exploit the available possibilities for improvement. For this reason the growth performance of firms, even those competing in the same market, may differ.

It is these features that we have tried to capture in our dynamic model of the growth of corporate productivity. The model captures the notions that technological progress and learning processes underlie the sustained growth of productivity and, as we shall demonstrate, profitability. But also that the magnitude of this growth is determined by a parameter reflecting corporate culture. We now proceed in Chapters 4–6 to present some applications of the model that has been constructed to actual data for companies and to analyse how the results can be used as an aid to management and to assist in long-term portfolio investment decisions.

APPENDIX 3.1   TECHNICAL DESCRIPTION OF THE MODEL OF CORPORATE PRODUCTIVITY

1   Formal description of the model[14]

Here we describe algebraically the model of corporate productivity growth. The model seeks to explain the evolution of the productive capacity of an enterprise or production unit in terms of changes in value added, defined by dA/dt, where t denotes time. We treat the productive unit, such as a plant, as a group of employees. Thus, A shows the share of each agent in the productive capacity of the plant, and output is considered in terms of value added per person. The reason for this is that the way in which an individual's productivity grows over time depends upon the manner in which he or she draws upon the technical knowledge and experience accumulated by all of the agents working in the production unit.

To incorporate the effects of swings and cycles in economic activity, the proportion of this productive capacity actually being exploited at a particular point in time, or the rate of capacity utilisation, M, is introduced into the model. In the standard approach to the growth of a firm it is steady-state outcomes that are concentrated upon and, therefore, the rate of capacity utilisation is treated as a constant. In this model M is a variable and is determined by fluctuations in the level of demand. So actual (annual) output per person, A^*M, is the product of actual productive capacity and the ability to utilise that capacity as dictated by demand conditions.

Revenues generated by the agents' participation in this production structure which exceed the level necessary for the enterprise to break even are assumed to be reinvested so as to increase his/her capacity to produce in the future

$$dA/dt = k_a * A * [M - M^*] \qquad (3.1)$$

where k_a is the capital–output ratio and M^* is the break-even level of utilisation of the plant or enterprise, where receipts are equal to total expenditures. The value of M^* is taken to be a function of actual productive capacity, A, and the maximum capacity that is feasible with a given technology, denoted by AL. To support this, assume away any cyclical fluctuations in demand so that $M = 1$. In this case $A = AL$, $M^* = 1$, and $dA/dt = 0$. In words, if the demand conditions permit capacity to be fully utilised, then the firm must produce the maximum amount from the available technology to break even. At the other extreme, it is clear that, with $M = 1$, if $AL = 0$ then $A = 0$. More generally we have

$$\lim A \to AL \text{ when } M^* \to 1$$

and

$$\lim A \to 0 \text{ when } M^* \to 0$$

On the basis of extensive empirical experimentation with firm-level data, the precise relationship between M^* and A is taken to be linear

$$M^* = A/AL \qquad (3.2)$$

When account is taken of cyclical variations in demand then $M < 1$ and so $A < AL$. If AL is constant (no technological change) then, from (3.1), it is the value of M that determines the amount that is to be invested each year and so the growth of capacity over time.

However, AL will change as technology changes. In this model technological advancement in the long run raises the level of AL and so lowers the level of M^*. Technical change increases the potential capacity of the firm which in turn reduces the amount of capacity required for the firm to break even. With a given level of actual capacity utilisation, this implies a greater surplus will be available for investment which will lead to a higher level of A. Thus, growth in potential capacity, AL, owing to changes in technology, permits growth in actual productive capacity, A.

We now introduce the experience effect and the innovation effect as the two factors responsible for the growth of AL. Here growth of the enterprise is linked to the cumulative value of output *within* the enterprise. In this model the experience relationship is entered as

$$dAL/AL = k_{sna} * (k_p * N * A)/(\Sigma k_p * N * A) \qquad (3.3)$$

where k_{sna} is a parameter, to be explained below, N is the total number of people employed in the market and where the summation in the denominator cumulates over time and production units, if there are more than one. The value of $N*A$ gives demand in the market under the assumption that the capacity of each agent to generate value added is similar in all the corporations competing in that market. The value of $k_p * N * A$, k_p reflecting the firm's market share, will be equal to the total capacity of the enterprise to produce value added which in turn will be equal to the product of the number of employees in the enterprise and productive capacity per employee, denoted by $pN * A$. So it is assumed that a firm's share of the market is equivalent to its share of the total number of workers in the sector, that is $pN = k_p * N$, the variable pN being the number of personnel necessary for the corporation to achieve a given share of non-cyclical market sales.

The experience effect derives from the cumulative value of (non-cyclical) output capacity of the enterprise as a whole. The growth of the productive potential of the individual depends upon the sum of the experience of all the employees of the enterprise. Production can be accumulated over time within the enterprise and over space, the latter being achieved, for example, through a merger.

Note that this specification of the experience effect abstracts from the impact of cyclical movements in demand and sales; experience depends upon the degree of productive capacity and not the rate at which that capacity is actually utilised. Other models have been developed which explicitly allow for the stock of knowledge to rise faster in cyclical upswings, when output is higher, than in recessions. However, empirical simulations show that in practice the effect of downswings on accumulated output are almost exactly offset by the impact of cyclical upswings, supporting the use of the trend value of capacity as the measure of experience.

The innovation effect shows how investment in (R & D) provides for new techniques by which productive potential may rise. In this model it is accumulated expenditures on R & D which influence the evolution of productive capacity

$$dAL/AL = k_{srd} * k_p * \Sigma RD \qquad (3.4)$$

The parameters, k_{sna} and k_{srd} in (3.3) and (3.4) show how changes in technology are translated into higher productive potential. The magnitude of this effect is a function of the corporate culture of the enterprise. The growth of an individual's productive potential depends upon the manner in which he or she draws upon the technical experience and knowledge acquired by all the agents working in the enterprise. This in turn is determined by their motivation, education, training and the general environment in which they work.

Bringing together the technological equations we obtain an expression for the evolution of maximum potential capacity per employee

$$dAL/dt = AL * [k_{sna} * (pN * A)/(\Sigma pN * A) + k_{srd} * k_p * \Sigma RD] \quad (3.5)$$

So the model predicts a long-run trend in technological progress, but unlike Solow the rate of technological change is determined by factors which are endogenous to the model. A key feature of the economic approach is the focus upon the profit-maximising firm run by rational economic beings. The principal determinants of long-term growth are the rate at which knowledge expands and the extent and speed to which it diffuses throughout the economy.

Here, as we discussed in more detail in Chapter 3, the underlying behavioural model is one of bounded rationality derived from an approach based upon cognitive psychology. The individual's potential capacity (AL) is less than the level that could be achieved from all the relevant information available, including the latest progress in technology. This limitation is a function of motivation, education, training and corporate culture. This implies differences between corporations in the effectiveness with which new technological opportunities are translated into actual increments in productive capacity.

Another of the basic variables in the model is the evolution of total employment in the sector relevant to the firm. To obtain an expression for the growth of employment we start by specifying the trend evolution of demand, $D(= N * A)$, as

$$dD/dt = k_{na} * D * (1 - D/DL) \qquad (3.6)$$

where DL reflects the level of potential demand in the market which grows at a constant rate

$$dDL/dt = k_{nal} * DL \qquad (3.7)$$

These equations generate an overall expansion path for the growth of demand of a product or market which has a logistic form. This allow us to express the evolution of the corresponding employment according to the relation:

$$d(N)/dt = k_{na}/A * (N * A(1 - A/AL) - NdA) \qquad (3.7')$$

The logistic approach provides the classical way of modelling the life-cycle of a particular product with the parameter k_{na} giving the rate of change of demand. Here we consider the firm and not the products of the firm individually. We are thus concerned with the evolution of demand for a range of products produced by the modern multi-product firm. The combination of these products is what we observe in the data. There is a mixture of new products, existing products and products which are close to the end of their lifecycle. This implies that the overall growth of demand for the output of the firm will follow the mature part of the logistic curve and this will evolve at the same rate as the potential capacity of the firm, defined by the growth coefficients for innovation and learning.

2 Empirical application of the model

Although elucidated in simple terms the model described above is computationally complex, involving non-linear dynamic, or differential, equations. To apply the model to actual data for corporations requires a simulation approach where the relevant parameter values are chosen on the basis of achieving a reasonable degree of fit with actual data for firms. In our previous work for a mainly academic business audience we have used a sophisticated modelling package and procedure.[15]

Given the richness of the model it is not possible to derive all the parameters by calibration. Thus most parameters are derived from the data while others are calibrated in the model on the basis of prior knowledge of plausible values. This permits attention to be focused on key parameters. These turn out to be the parameters in the 'technology equations' which determine the relative importance of the experience effect and the innovation effect and those determining the evolution of demand. The criterion used in selecting the values of these key parameters is to minimise the sum of the squared errors. Overall the model is evaluated in terms of its ability to limit the error of prediction at each observation to within 5 per cent of the actual value.

The model is applied to data of value added for a range of corporations for a minimum of a 10-year period. What is observed is the value of $M*A$, actual output per person employed. In other words, the data include both the long-run trend and the cyclical components of the change in the individual's productivity. In the sophisticated modelling approach these separate effects are isolated by adopting a simultaneous two-stage approach to the simulation exercise.

First, the model is used to predict the long-run trend evolution of value added per person holding the level of capacity utilisation constant. In this stage it is the technological factors, the experience effect and the innovation effect which determine the rate of growth of productive capacity – that is, the variable A. The parameters in the technological equations are chosen to minimise the error between the predicted value of $M*A$ and the observed value in the data. At the same time the value of A is used to establish the trend value of demand using (3.4) and (3.5). The model generates a predicted value for the number of employees, pN, which is compared with the actual number of agents in the enterprise.

As the parameters of this trend stage of the exercise are calibrated, an estimate is simultaneously provided from a second stage of the cyclical value added per person, which is compared with the actual data. This second stage provides a value of capacity utilisation, M, which has to be applied to the estimate of A from the trend stage to replicate the data. Again, these values are fed into the model of demand to derive an estimate of the number of persons employed, which is compared with the actual data on employment. An iterative procedure then follows with parameter values being adjusted so as to minimise the errors between the actual and predicted values of value added per person and the number of persons employed.

In a cyclical economy observed value added varies because of changes in the rate of capacity utilisation. This rate of capacity utilisation reflects both changes in price and volume of production. However, in many cases the rate of capacity utilisation predicted by the model appears to represent very well the economic environment faced by firms in a particular market. To support this assertion consider Figures 3A.1–3A.3, which compare the simulated values of capacity utilisation for firms competing within the same market. The analysis is provided for three cases of different economic and market conditions. The figures clearly suggest a common trend in capacity utilisation among firms competing in the same market, this being more pronounced for the chemicals than for the electronics firms. Both these pieces of information thus support the notion that, in general, the interface between the firm and the cyclical environment in which it operates is adequately represented by the simulated degree of capacity utilisation, M. However, where the correlation between the estimated

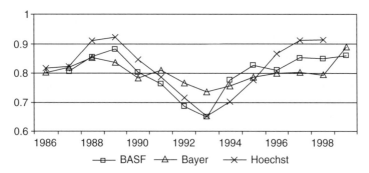

Figure 3A.1   Utilisation rate of selected German chemicals firms, 1986–98

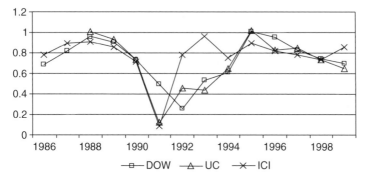

Figure 3A.2   Utilisation rate of other selected chemicals firms, 1986–98

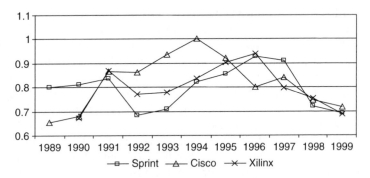

Figure 3A.3   Utilisation rate of selected electronics firms, 1989–99

trend and the actual data is very low results are treated with a great deal of caution. This suggests that the firm is subject to large cyclical swings in productivity.

The approach described above has been applied using quite sophisticated software. However, a slightly more simple approach can be implemented using standard spreadsheets to estimate the growth coefficients for each of the main variables. This is the method that we adopt for some of the data applications in this book, such as the portfolio analysis of Chapter 6. Further, in some cases data on R&D expenditures are not available so that we are unable separately to identify the experience effect and the technology effect as the key factors pushing forward the technological possibilities of the firm. In this case we estimate a single technological parameter (which we define as k_{al}) which captures both experience and innovation effects. This means that we cannot identify firms in which growth is based more on learning than innovation, or vice versa, as we have done in previous exercises. However, the more simple approach here does not in any way detract from the overall analysis of growth of productivity that is presented in Chapters 4–6. This assertion is based upon comparisons of the simple approach with the more sophisticated modelling which separately identifies the technological and learning effects for firms where R & D data are available. Most of the analysis in this book will be identical to that provided by the more sophisticated approach.

APPENDIX 3.2   THE CALIBRATION OF THE MODEL

The key variables of attention in the calibration of the model are:

- the growth of value added per head (productivity)
- the evolution of the number of employees
- the trend in wages and salaries
- the long-term growth rate of operating profits.

We now turn to give a brief description of how the model is calibrated to allow analysis of these key variables. Box 3A.1 provides a step-by-step overview of the process of calibrating the model.

We have chosen a particular but unnamed company as a good example of the way that the model is calibrated. We start the analysis by calculating the (exponential) coefficient of the growth of value added per head (the parameter k_{al}) during the period considered, which is typically from 1985 to 1999. This is done by simple linear

---

Box 3A.1   The calibration procedure for the model

Trend module

1. Calculate the exponential coefficient of the trend growth of value added per head and the initial value of the trend of value added per head.
2. Calculate the exponential coefficient of the trend growth of wages per head and the initial value of the trend of wages per head.
3. Calculate the exponential coefficient of the trend growth of employment (in some cases, it is necessary to consider several trends over the time period).
4. Set the initial value of the market share, in terms of the share of employment of the firm in relation to its sectors of activities
5. Calibrate the capital ratio parameter by a comparison of the data on the rate of return on investment and the rate of return calculated by the model.
6. Set the initial trend value of the rate of utilisation (typically around 0.8).
7. Calibrate the initial value of the ratio A/AL through the fitting of the growth of A with the growth of AL.

Cyclical module

The cyclical module is automatically calibrated by the integration of the difference between the data and the trend in the calculation of the simulated cyclical value added per head.

regression analysis with the natural logarithm of the data on value added per head being regressed against time.[16] The parameter on time gives the exponential growth coefficient. Figure 3A.4 gives the result of this procedure for the chosen company, showing the actual data for value added per head together with the estimated trend. The same approach is also applied to estimate the exponential coefficient of the growth of wages per head (k_{salm}).

We also present on Figure 3A.4 the estimated value of the growth coefficient, in this case 6.6 per cent, and the value of the correlation coefficient, R^2. The latter statistic provides a measure of the reliability of the estimate of the trend. It shows how much of the variation over time in productivity or profits is explained by the trend approach. In this case, the correlation coefficient is very high, suggesting that for this firm, 97 per cent of the variation in value added per head over the 15-year period can be explained by the trend.

In a cyclical economy observed value added varies because of changes in the rate of capacity utilisation and because of possible cyclical price changes. As discussed in Appendix 3.1, for the majority of firms the rate of capacity utilisation predicted by the model appears to represent very well the economic environment faced by the firm in the relevant market. The difference between the data and the estimated trend of value added per person can be associated with the rate of capacity utilisation of the firm.

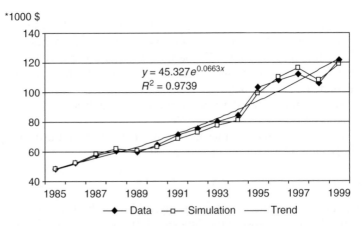

Figure 3A.4 Estimated trend, data and simulated value of (deflated) value added per head for a representative firm, 1985–99

However, in general, it is much more difficult to define a trend for firms which are greatly affected by cyclical swings in the economy. This is something to which we return in Chapter 6 when we discuss how our approach here might provide useful information when choosing firms for a long-run investment portfolio. The accuracy of our approach will be much lower in cases where the trend explains only a small proportion of the variation over time in the key variables.

By combining the information on the growth coefficient for wages and salaries with that regarding the growth of productivity we are able to derive a growth coefficient for operating profits (earnings before interest, taxes, depreciation and amortisation, or EBITDA) per head.[17] The actual data and the predicted trend for our chosen company are shown in Figure 3A.5. The other main variable in the model is the growth of the number of employees. Figure 3A.6 plots the actual data, the fitted trend and the predicted values for employment for the chosen company.

In the case of some companies, in contrast to the evolution of value added per head, it is difficult to define a single growth coefficient for employment during the whole period. Productivity growth, which is fundamentally linked to technological change, appears to evolve at a much more constant rate over time. However, the impact of restructuring or mergers or the sale of a part of the firm can lead to considerable variations in the short run in the number of employees. Where this problem arises we have calculated growth coefficients for the number of employees over different, well-defined, sub-periods and then calculated the growth rate for the whole of the period considered as an average of the growth coefficients in each subperiod.

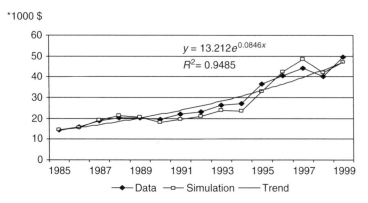

Figure 3A.5   Estimated trend, data and stimulated value of (deflated) operating profit per head for a chosen firm, 1985–99

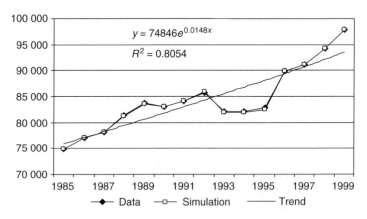

Figure 3A.6   Estimated trend, data and simulated value of number of employees for a representative company, 1985–99

Finally, we combine the trend in gross profits per head with the evolution of the number of employees to obtain the trend in overall operating profits (EBITDA) (see Figure 3A.7).

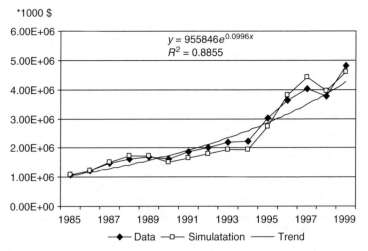

Figure 3A.7   Estimated trend, data and simulated value of (deflated) gross profitability for a representative company, 1985–99

4 Application of the Model as a Management Tool

4.1 INTRODUCTION

In this chapter we proceed to apply the model and ideas presented in Chapter 3 to data for actual companies. We consider a range of companies in the following major sectors; chemicals, pharmaceuticals and electronics. All of the data are derived from annual company accounts and come from publicly accessible internet sites.[1] We present a simple application of the model, the details of the calibration of the model are described in Appendices 3.1 and 3.2 (pp. 39–50).

Chapter 3 showed that modern multi-product firms tend to exhibit sustained and constant growth of productivity. The aim of the empirical model is to identify the growth coefficient of productivity, defined as average value added per employee. This is then combined with an analysis of the trend in the growth of average wages and salaries, in profit per person, and the evolution of the number of employees. We first show how these outputs from the model can be used to define and compare the performance of different corporations and how this can be used within a company to assess existing and potential strategies. We believe that by looking at the long-run or trend evolution of key variables important information can be gleaned which will demonstrate more clearly the strengths and weaknesses of a particular company and its proposed strategies, in relation to the market in which the firm competes. We then proceed in Chapter 5 to an analysis of the impact of mergers.

The key issue for firms is how to sustain the growth of profits over time. Throughout our analysis we will refer to operating profits or EBITDA (see p. 49) as the main variable of attention for the firm. As we suggested in Chapter 2, firms make investment decisions on the basis of increasing profits in the long run, while profits provide for future investment. Hence, profits are a necessary condition for growth. However, we will show that growth of profits is strongly correlated with the growth rate of productivity. This reinforces the point made earlier that in the long run the growth of profitability and the growth of productivity are synonymous. This follows from the fact that the trend in the growth of operating profit for the firm is determined by:

1. the trend in operating profit per employee
2. the evolution of the number of employees.

In other words, overall operating profits can increase if the number of employees increases (the number of actors generating profits per head) or the amount of operating profit per employee rises. For given levels of wages, growth of operating profit per head results from rising value added per head, which in turn reflects improvements in productivity over time. This leads us to classify firms where the trend in the growth of operating profits emanates primarily from rising numbers of employees as exhibiting strong performance in sales and marketing, while firms whose trend growth of operating profits is primarily due to rising productivity are classed as firms with a strong technological performance.

4.2   ANALYSIS OF CHEMICALS AND PHARMACEUTICALS FIRMS

We start by presenting an analysis of the chemicals and pharmaceuticals industries. Later we will look at the electronics industry. We consider the performance of chemicals and pharmaceuticals companies together because several firms are currently active in both sectors and so we distinguish between firms which are primarily involved in producing chemicals, firms which are mainly oriented towards pharmaceuticals products and firms which are classified as mixed chemicals–pharmaceuticals.

Market growth in the chemicals sector has been slow relative to that of pharmaceuticals and this has constrained the growth potential of individual firms and hence the possibility for rapid expansion of profits. As a result a number of chemicals firms have commenced a transition into pharmaceuticals activities to avoid the straightjacket of a low level of market and technological potential.[2]

We start by showing for 23 of the main chemicals and pharmaceuticals companies the average of the trend growth in employment, plotted on the vertical axis in Figure 4.1, against the trend growth in operating profit per head, plotted on the horizontal axis in the figure. The combination of these two variables gives the growth in overall

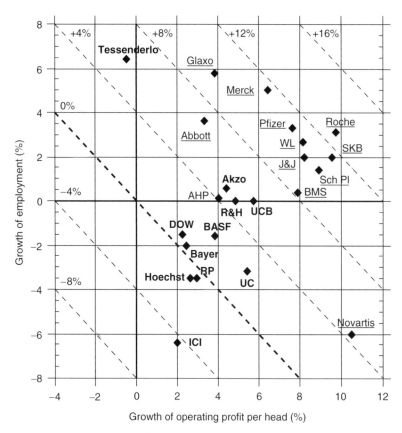

Figure 4.1   Scatter of growth of operating profit per head and growth of employment in chemicals and pharmaceticals firms

Note: **Tessenderlo** = Chemicals firm.
AHP = Chemico–pharmaceuticals firm.
<u>Glaxo</u> = Pharmaceuticals firm.

gross profitability since, by definition, overall operating profit (EBITDA) equals operating profit per head multiplied by the number of employees.

   We loosely identify three types of firms:

- *Chemicals firms*: Akzo Nobel, DOW Chemical, ICI, Rhom & Haas (R&H), Tessenderlo, Union Carbide (UC)
- *Mixed chemico–pharmaceuticals firms*: American Home Products (AHP), BASF, Bayer, Hoechst, Rhône-Poulenc (RP), Union Chimique Belge (UCB)

- *Pharmaceuticals firms*: Abbott Labs, Bristol-Myers Squibb (BMS), Glaxo Wellcome, Johnson&Johnson (J&J), Merck, Novartis, Pfizer, Roche, SmithKline Beecham (SKB), Schering-Plough (Sch Pl), Warner-Lambert (WL).

The mixed firms are classified as those in transition from the chemicals to the pharmaceuticals sector where a significant amount of sales now come from pharmaceuticals products. This is not a definitive break-down and is drawn up primarily on the basis of an understanding of the market rather than strict statistical definitions. In Figure 4.1 the chemicals firms are shown in bold type, the mixed chemico–pharma-ceuticals firms are shown in normal type and the pharmaceuticals firms are underlined.

The dotted diagonal lines in Figure 4.1 show different levels of growth of overall operating profits. Companies located in the upper right-hand quadrant exhibit positive average growth of operating profits which results from both growth of operating profit per head and growth of employment. It is apparent that most of the pharmaceuticals companies are located in this quadrant of the figure. The lower right-hand quad-rant, where most of the chemicals and chemico–pharmaceuticals com-panies are located, shows positive growth of operating profits per head but a decline, on average, in employment in these companies. Within this group companies located above the diagonal line marked 0 have experi-enced positive growth of profitability (the decline in employment is more than offset by the increase in profits per head). For firms below this diagonal line the increase in operating profit per head has been insuffi-cient to ensure a positive trend in the growth of overall operating profits.

The upper left-hand quadrant shows positive growth of employment with declining profits per head. For firms located above the diagonal line marked with 0, growth of operating profits is positive. Only one firm is situated in this area. The final quadrant shows negative employment growth, negative growth of operating profit per head and therefore a decline in overall profitability. None of the sampled firms in the chemi-cals and pharmaceuticals industries reflects this type of performance.

More specifically we also observe that almost all the firms present a positive growth of operating profit per head. However, most of the chemicals firms and the mixed chemico–pharmaceuticals companies exhibit positive operating profit per head growth but a decline in employ-ment growth. In fact the chemicals firms are characterised by two clear trends in employment which, as briefly discussed in Appendix 3.2 (p. 49), are allowed for in the calibration of the model. There was moderate growth in employment in the 1980s with a stronger trend decline in the 1990s. The latter effect dominates in the averages that underlie Figure 4.1. Pharmaceuticals firms reflect a single upward trend in employment throughout the whole of the period. Most of the pharmaceuticals firms, and particularly the older, more established companies (Glaxo, Pfizer), show both a positive trend in the growth of operating profit per head and on average employment growth. It appears that the pharmaceuticals firms are characterised by a much higher trend rate of growth of operating profit (more than 5 per cent) than the chemicals firms.[3]

The analysis of Figure 4.1 also leads to a distinction between firms whose growth is based primarily upon the increase in productivity and those firms which are able to raise the number of employees by their performance in the market – in other words, through their success in marketing and selling. Figure 4.1 shows that for most of the firms in these two sectors growth is primarily driven by increases in productivity. Nevertheless, some firms (such as Tessenderlo, Glaxo and Abbott Labs) present a rather low growth of operating profit per head but a strong increase in employment, reflecting a more market oriented strategy with less emphasis on productivity growth. We suggest that the growth of operating profit per head may be taken as an indicator of the technological success of the firm. In our approach, technological advancement captures the introduction of new techniques and technologies but also the benefits from learning by doing, which is becoming so important in the knowledge economy. The impact of both of these technological factors are revealed in increasing levels of labour productivity, as reflected in the growth of value added per head and, for a given evolution of wages, in the growth of operating profit per head. The growth of employment is interpreted as an indicator of the success of the company in marketing and selling. Given the growth of operating profits per employee, as determined by technological performance, companies can increase total operating profits by raising the number of employees. This in turn requires success in selling in the market.

4.2.1   Analysis of the trend in operating profit

We now look in more detail at the performance of firms within these sectors, in terms of the trend rate of growth of operating profits per head. In all of the figures which follow in this chapter the data, and the estimated trend values, have been deflated by the relevant national price deflator. In Figures 4.2, 4.3 and 4.4 we look separately at firms in the chemicals sector, mixed chemico–pharmaceuticals firms, and then pharmaceuticals firms. Subsequently we will look at the growth of value added per head and the growth of wages and salaries for these groups of firms. In Chapter 6 we will consider carefully the correlation between our performance measure, growth of operating profit, and the market value of the firm, which suggests that our analysis provides useful information for long-term portfolio investment decisions.

Figure 4.2 plots the trend in operating profit per employee for the chemicals firms, and shows in addition to the growth of operating profit the initial and final levels of operating profits per head for each firm. This allows us to assess whether those firms which are currently the most profitable are also those which registered the fastest growth of profits over the 15-year period from 1985 to 1999. Alternatively, we can see whether there has been a degree of catching-up with those enterprises showing low initial profits experiencing fast growth.[4]

The evidence from Figure 4.2 is rather mixed, although there is clearly no strong evidence of convergence. If anything, these chemicals firms display a tendency towards increasing divergence in absolute levels of gross profitability. In general those firms with low levels of initial operating profit per head tended to increase profits at a slower rate than those chemicals firms with initially high profits per head. However, there are exceptions as shown by Akzo, which had the lowest level of initial profits but registered higher than average growth, and R&H and UC, which grew faster than DOW, the firm with the highest profit per head in 1985.

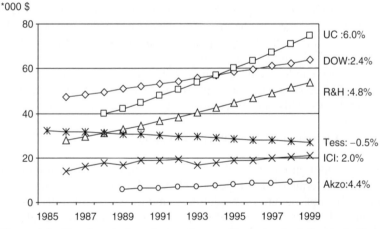

Figure 4.2   Trend evolution of operating profit per head of chemicals firms 1985–99

Figures 4.3 and 4.4 present the same analysis for the mixed chemico–pharmaceuticals firms and the pharmaceuticals firms. The figures show that, in general, the pharmaceuticals firms have a higher absolute level of operating profit per head than the chemicals companies and substantially higher than the mixed chemico–pharmaceuticals firms. The top three chemicals firms (UC, DOW and R&H) generate operating profit per head of a comparable magnitude to the average pharmaceuticals firm.

The firms in a transition state from a chemicals to a predominantly pharmaceuticals company all have a level of operating profit per head less than the lowest of the pharmaceuticals firms. The figures also suggest that the growth rate of operating profit is generally higher for the pharmaceuticals firms than for the chemicals firms. The growth of profits for the mixed chemico–pharmaceuticals firms tends to be slightly higher than the average for the chemicals firms but still substantially below the average for the pharmaceuticals firms.

The data in the previous Figures 4.2–4.4 suggest a general relationship between the current level of operating profit per head and the trend rate of growth of operating profit per head over the previous period. Firms with a high level of operating profit per head have also tended to grow at a faster rate that firms with lower levels of profitability. This implies that the firms which have exhibited the fastest

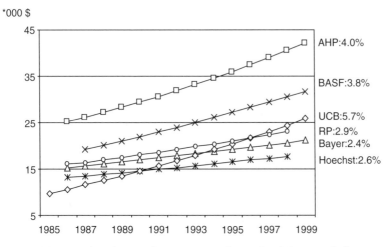

Figure 4.3   Trend evolution of operating profit per head for mixed chemico–pharmaceuticals firms, 1985–99

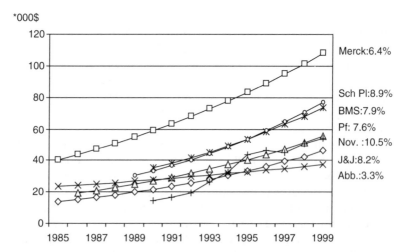

Figure 4.4   Trend evolution of operating profit per head for pharmaceuticals firms, 1985–99

growth of profitability were also those with relatively high levels of profits per head at the start of the period. This provides some evidence that history matters and that long-run trend behaviour tends to be extended into the future.

We continue along these lines in Figure 4.5, where we plot the growth of operating profit per head against the value of operating profit per head in 1999, as given by the trend value. This confirms the broad suggestion that firms with currently high levels of operating profit per head tended to exhibit higher levels of growth of operating profit per head over the previous 10-year period. However, again there is quite a high degree of variation among the firms in this sample. Again, most of the pharmaceuticals companies are located in the north-east part of the figure, reflecting strong growth and a high current value of operating profit per head, while Figure 4.6 shows a similar picture for total operating profits.

4.2.2   Analysis of the trend in productivity

We now turn to look at the evolution of productivity, as measured by value added per person, and, following the approach in Figures 4.5 and 4.6, we compact the information into a single graph, Figure 4.7. The graph plots the trend growth of productivity along the horizontal axis

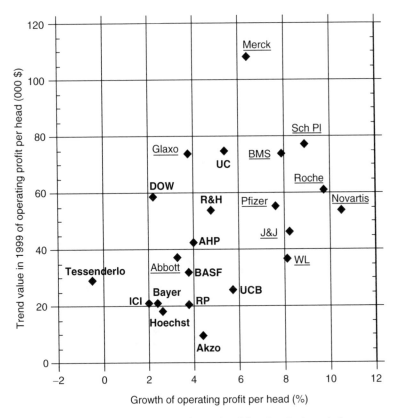

Figure 4.5   Growth of operating profit per head for chemicals and pharmaceuticals firms, 1985–99

against the (trend) value of productivity in 1999. Figure 4.7 suggests that those firms which are currently the most productive, in terms of having high values of value added per head in 1999, are also the firms where productivity grew fastest over the previous 15-year period. It is worth noting that the location of companies in Figure 4.7 is very similar to that of Figure 4.1, with the pharmaceuticals firms showing the highest trend rate of productivity growth.

Excluding Tessenderlo, which as we saw from Figure 4.1 appears to have been following a market oriented strategy which is quite distinct from other firms in the sector, the range of growth coefficients of value added per head for the chemicals firms lie between 2.2 and 4 per cent. This compares with the range of the growth coefficients of the growth

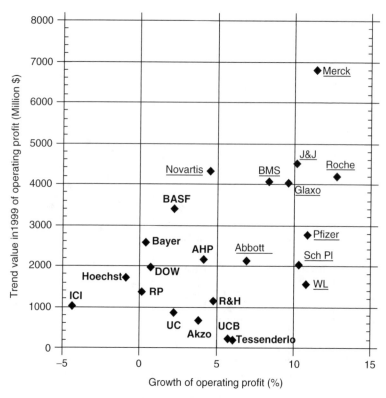

Figure 4.6   Growth of operating profit for chemicals and pharmaceuticals firms

of operating profit per head, shown in Figure 4.2, of 2–6 per cent (again excluding Tessenderlo).

With the exception of Abbott, all of the pharmaceuticals firms have much higher *levels* of productivity than the chemicals firms and the mixed chemico–pharmaceuticals companies. Interestingly, the productivity levels of the mixed firms fall in the middle of the range of the productivity levels of the chemicals companies. With regard to the *growth* of productivity, again, the pharmaceuticals companies have been able to expand productivity at much faster rates than the chemicals and mixed companies. The simple average growth rate across the pharmaceuticals companies is around 5 per cent per annum, while the average for the chemicals firms is 2.8 per cent and for the mixed firms it is 2.7 per cent.

Thus, these results suggest that growth possibilities, in terms of both productivity improvements and increases in profit per head, are much

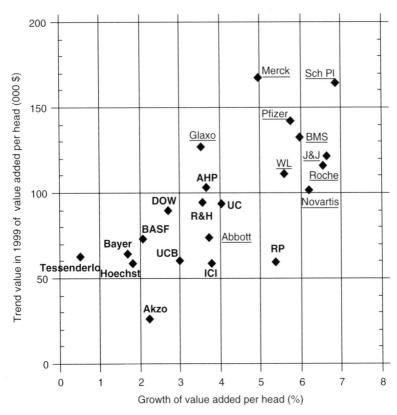

Figure 4.7 Growth of value added per head for chemicals and pharmaceuticals firms

more limited in the chemicals sector than in the pharmaceuticals market. This reflects the role of technological opportunities and potential development of the market in affecting growth opportunities for firms. In the model this is reflected in the rigidity of the growth coefficient of productivity, which in turn determines the growth of profits per employee, given developments in wages, to which we turn next. Finally, it is worth noting that those firms which have sought to loosen the straightjacket of low growth opportunities in the chemicals market by increasing their involvement in pharmaceuticals activities have yet to register performance substantially different from the chemicals firms. This suggests that it may take many years for the chemicals firms to attain the productivity levels and the growth coefficients of the pharmaceuticals firms.

In general, these results suggest that those firms which at present exhibit the highest levels of operating profits and productivity per head have typically experienced the fastest rates of growth of profitability and productivity over the previous period. This implies that at the start of the period these firms were also the most profitable and productive. These results thus suggest that history does matter and that firms which have grown strongly in the past will have in place a corporate environment which will be conducive to future growth of profitability per head and productivity.

4.2.3 Analysis of the trend in wages and salaries

Figure 4.8 shows the trend rate of growth of wages per employee for the three groups of firms and the level of wages per head in 1999. Again

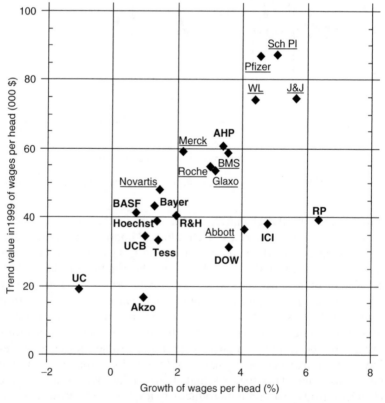

Figure 4.8   Growth of wages per head for chemicals and pharmaceuticals firms

with the exception of Abbott, the pharmaceuticals firms pay much higher wages and salaries on average than do the chemicals and mixed firms, and so are much better able to attract and retain the more able and more productive workers in the workforce. Given the role of the individual in the growth process of the firm, in terms of learning by doing, this suggests that those firms which are able to attract the most able workers are more likely to experience faster rates of productivity increase. This in turn will enable these firms to afford to offer relatively high increases in wages and salaries over time. There is thus likely to be a strong correlation between productivity growth and the growth of wages and salaries, a feature which will be confirmed later in the chapter after we have analysed firm performance in another sector, the electronics sector.

4.3 ANALYSIS OF ELECTRONICS FIRMS

We now provide a similar analysis of firms in the electronics sector, a sector which has very different propensities to the pharmaceuticals and particularly the chemicals sector. Electronics is a relatively new and very fast-growing sector and so it is of interest to see whether the model of corporate productivity growth that we have developed appears to be of relevance here, as well as to mature sectors such as chemicals and pharmaceuticals. Because of this fast growth the axes in Figure 4.9 are of a quite different magnitude to those in Figure 4.1, for the chemicals and pharmaceuticals firms.

Figure 4.9 shows that, with the exception of Sprint and Compaq after its merger with DEC (this will be discussed in more detail in Chapter 5), most firms exhibit positive trend growth of profitability per head. For most of the firms this rate of growth of profitability per head is considerably higher that the average for the chemicals and pharmaceuticals firms. Again there is some variation across these electronics firms in the extent to which growth of overall operating profits is generated by technological strength, as reflected in the increase in profitability per head, and/or by marketing and sales abilities, as shown by the rate of growth of employment. For firms such as Ericsson, Altera and Intel, growth of overall operating profits has been primarily due to technological performance. Microsoft and Dell demonstrate that growth of profits is due to a mixture of strong performance in technology and in selling. For Cisco, which appears somewhat exceptional, it is performance in selling and

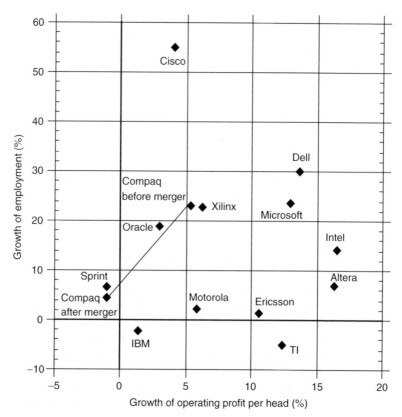

Figure 4.9   Scatter of growth of operating profit per head and growth of employment in electronics firms

marketing which has been the principle source of the growth of overall profitability.

Figures 4.10 and 4.11 plot the trend rate of growth of operating profits per head against time for the electronics firms. Here the relationship between current levels of profitability and the rate of growth of profitability is less clear than in the case of the chemicals and pharmaceuticals firms. This reflects the fact that some of the firms have a relatively short history and the industry itself is much less mature. This is further shown in Figure 4.12 which plots the rate of growth of operating profits per head against the trend level of profit per head in 1999. Again, there is some tendency for the firms with currently the highest levels of profits per head to have shown

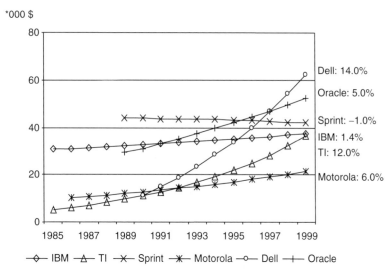

Figure 4.10 Trend evolution of operating profit per head for electronics firms, 1985–99: 1

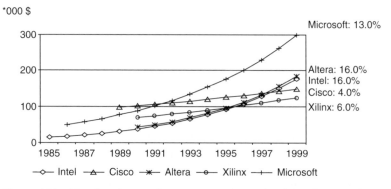

Figure 4.11 Trend evolution of operating profit per head for electrnics firms, 1985–99: 2

relatively fast growth of profits per head, such as Microsoft, Altera, Intel, Cisco and Xilinx. However, there are exceptions. Dell, Texas Instruments (TI) and Ericsson have all shown higher than average growth of operating profits per head, but still have relatively low levels of profits.

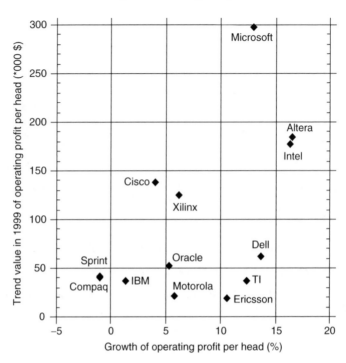

Figure 4.12   Growth of operating profit per head for electronics firms

Figure 4.13 shows the relationship between current levels of productivity and the trend growth of productivity over the previous period for which data is available. Again the most productive firms in 1999, Microsoft, Altera and Intel, also experienced the fastest rates of productivity growth. Cisco exhibits a high level of productivity but relatively slow growth of value added per head over the previous period, again suggesting that this company has concentrated more on selling and marketing than upon technological performance in recent years. Some firms, such as Ericsson and TI, demonstrate relatively strong growth of productivity but have levels of productivity substantially below those of the more advanced firms in the sector.

Finally, in Figure 4.14 we look at the relationship between the current trend level of average wages and salaries and the trend growth of worker remuneration. In general, those firms with higher productivity and higher profitability tend to pay higher wages and salaries on average, and these companies typically demonstrate faster rates of growth of wages. An exception is clearly Oracle where the level of

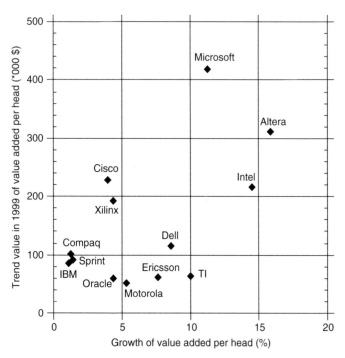

Figure 4.13   Growth of value added per head for electronics firms

average wages and salaries in 1999 was very low compared to other firms in the sector. In addition, the trend in the growth of wages and salaries has been negative for this company. Thus, the growth in its operating profit per head has been generated partly from this trend decline in wages and salaries. In the following section we discuss whether, in the long term, firms will be able to sustain productivity and profit growth while providing a trend growth in wages and salaries which is substantially below the growth of productivity.

4.4   THE RELATIONSHIP BETWEEN GROWTH OF PRODUCTIVITY AND GROWTH OF WAGES AND SALARIES PER HEAD

Before proceeding further to an application of the model to an analysis of alternative management scenarios we need to draw attention to the important links between productivity growth and the growth of wages

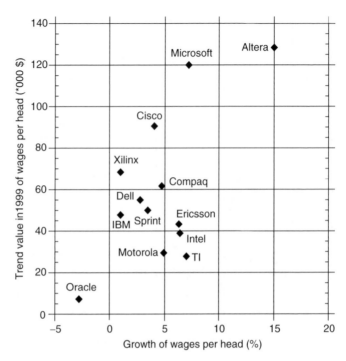

Figure 4.14   Growth of wages per head for electronics firms

of the individual. Figure 4.15, for chemicals and pharmaceuticals firms, and Figure 4.16, for electronics firms, present the correlation between the trend growth of productivity and the growth coefficient for wages and salaries per head.

It is clear that for both of these samples of firms there is a positive relationship between the growth of productivity and the growth of wages and salaries. On the one hand, since the growth of operating profit per head is given by the difference between the growth of value added per head, productivity and the growth of wages and salaries per head, sustained growth of wages and salaries will be possible only if productivity is growing. By definition, if wages and salaries grow faster than productivity then operating profit per head will decline. Hence, firms will be able to accommodate consistent growth of wages and salaries per head only if there is sustained growth of productivity. On the other hand, there is also causality in the opposite direction. Firms will be able to keep and attract the most

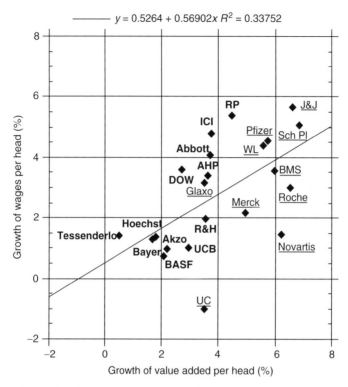

Figure 4.15 Correlation between growth of productivity and growth of wages per head for chemicals and pharmaceuticals firms

able workers only if they offer the prospects of continual increases in individual wages and salaries.

As we have argued elsewhere in this book, the quality of workers and the way that they interact within the firm plays a crucial role in determining the rate of productivity growth. Hence, firms which do not offer rising wages and salaries are unlikely to be able to sustain significant productivity growth in the medium to long-term.

The slope of the straight line in Figures 4.15 and 4.16 shows the precise estimated relationship between productivity growth and growth of wages and salaries. The estimated equation which defines this line is shown above the graph.[5] Thus for chemicals and pharmaceuticals firms on average, an increase in the trend rate of growth of productivity by 1 per cent is associated with an increase in the trend growth of wages and salaries of 0.57 per cent. For the electronics firms

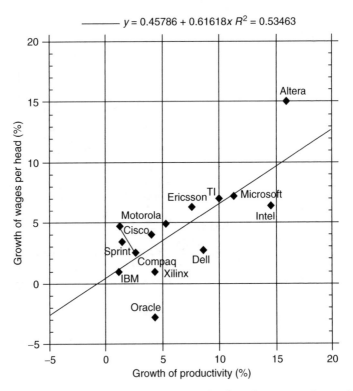

Figure 4.16   Correlation between the growth of productivity and growth of wages per head for electronics firms

the slope of the line is very similar. A 1 per cent increase in the growth rate of productivity is associated with a 0.61 per cent increase in wages and salaries. Given the two-way causality between these variables, we may also say that a 1 per cent increase in the rate of growth of wages and salaries is, on average, associated with a 1.75 per cent increase in the rate of growth of productivity for chemicals and pharmaceuticals firms, and a 1.64 per cent increase for electronics firms.

Of course, these are statements about relationships on average. However, we may also suggest that firms which are substantially above the estimated line are unlikely to be able to sustain strong growth of operating profits per head since the growth of wages and salaries will be close to or above the rate of growth of productivity. Firms which lie substantially below the line, while generating strong growth of operating profits per head, by offering relatively slow growth of wages and salaries are likely to face difficulties in keeping and attracting the best staff, which will compromise attempts to sustain productivity growth in the future.

4.5 ANALYSIS OF BUSINESS PLANS[6]

The model and approach to the firm developed here can be used to analyse various aspects of the business plan of a corporation or units within a firm. The model can be used to assess the coherence of the projections for the main variables of the business plan, employment, production and profitability, and also to evaluate its feasibility in terms of the consistency between the plan and the trend values of the relevant variables. The model can also be used in the process of developing the business plan. For example, the business unit may start with a forecast for the level of activity or expected production that is envisaged. If there is a high degree of confidence in the ability successfully to place this output on the market, then the predicted trend growth of productivity will permit a forecast of the required allocation of manpower under the plan.

More generally, the model provides an estimate of the trend rate of growth of productivity arising from R&D activities and from learning processes, the magnitude of the growth coefficient being influenced by the corporate culture of the firm and the external environment in which the firm operates – specifically, the rate of growth of demand for the products that the firm produces. The model inherently obliges managers to take into account the implications of the rigidity that the coefficient of the growth of the trend of value added per head imposes on management. In the short to medium term productivity cannot be improved at a considerably faster rate than is dictated by this coefficient.

The approach to analysing business plans could equally be applied to different units within a firm, if data on value added, employment and operating profit were available. This would allow a judgement of the feasibility of the proposals for each of the units, together with a view of their consistency with the business plan for the corporation as a whole.

We proceed to demonstrate these issues by a hypothetical analysis of various scenarios for a particular, representative, firm as a whole. We briefly illustrate how the analysis of the trend performance of a company, which we have developed in this book, can be used to assess the potential impact of alternative scenarios for the firm. We address separately two issues, first how different assumptions about the economic environment can affect projections of the future evolution of productivity and profitability in relation to the long-run trend growth values for these variables. Secondly, we show how changes in the trend rates of growth of employment and average wages affect the projected growth of operating profits, for given productivity growth.

4.5.1 The impact of different assumptions concerning the economic environment

We start by looking at the impact of different conjectures concerning the economic environment, which are integrated into the model via different choices for the future evolution of the utilization rate of the firm. Here the scenarios are based upon the calibrated values from actual data, covering the period 1985–99, for a representative firm. We consider two scenarios for the evolution of the rate of utilisation:

- In scenario 1 (conservative scenario) the future evolution of the utilisation rate is based upon an extension of the previous pattern over the past 15 years.
- In scenario 2 (optimistic scenario) a higher and more favourable rate of utilisation is assumed for the following period.

The assumptions concerning the utilisation rate are shown in Figure 4.17. In both scenarios it is assumed that the change in employment

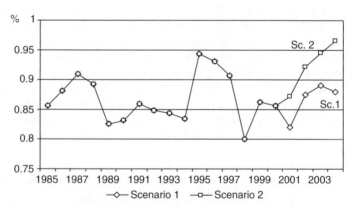

Figure 4.17   Scenarios of the utilisation rate for a representative firm, 1985–2003

continues along its trend path, in this case an annual increase of 3.5 per cent per annum. The simulation of the model provides a prediction of the future evolution of value added per head, operating profits per head and overall operating profits (given the assumption concerning employment growth) for the two scenarios.

Figures 4.18 and 4.19 present the projected evolution of productivity and profitability, respectively, under the two scenarios. Under scenario 1 both productivity and profitability evolve around the trend value derived from simply extrapolating forward the calibrated growth

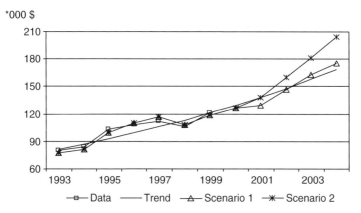

Figure 4.18 Evolution of value added per head for a representative firm under alternative scenarios, 1993–2003

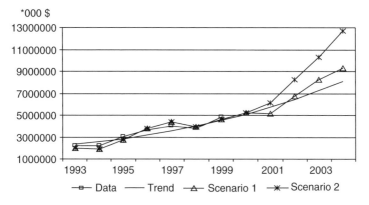

Figure 4.19 Evolution of operating profit for a representative firm under alternative scenarios, 1993–2003

coefficient. Scenario 2 presents the classical 'hockey stick effect' which can be typical in business plans and entails an evolution far from the trend value. The application of the model thus permits an assessment of the implications of assumptions regarding the economic environment which underlie business plans. More specifically, the model shows whether predicted values for productivity and profitability are coherent and consistent with previous patterns of the economic environment that the particular firm has experienced.

4.5.2 Scenarios of different assumptions concerning growth of employment and growth of wages

Here we consider a firm characterised by a trend growth rate of productivity of 4.5 per cent per annum (as shown in Figure 4.20) and growth of wages per head of 5 per cent. The firm has experienced a period of restructuring whereby two trends in employment are apparent, the first (between 1986 and 1990) is represented by a trend increase of 4.5 per cent per year, while the second period (1991–9) shows a trend rate of decline in employment of 4 per cent per annum. This profile, which is clearly shown for our representative firm in Figure 4.21, has been observed for most of the chemicals firms in our sample during the period 1985–99. These features define the reference scenario, Figure 4.22 shows that under these conditions operating profits grew at an annual average rate of 1.4 per cent across the whole of the period.

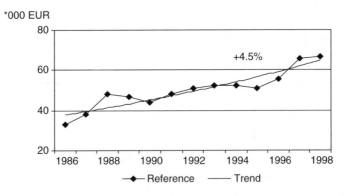

Figure 4.20 Trend growth of value added per head of a representative firm, 1986–98

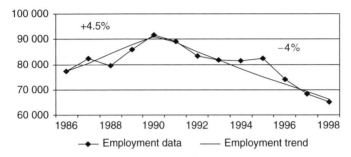

Figure 4.21   Evolution of the employment of a representative firm, 1986–98

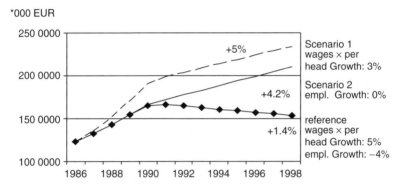

Figure 4.22   Impact of scenarios on trend of operating profit for a representative firm, 1986–98

We now consider how different evolutions of employment and wages would have affected the growth of operating profit, taking as given the growth of productivity. We consider two alternative scenarios:

• wages per head grew at a rate of 3 per cent instead of 5 per cent
• employment remained constant since 1990 instead of declining by 4 per cent on average each year after that date.

The results, which are shown in Figure 4.22, suggest that the period of restructuring had a significant affect on the growth of operating profit. If this firm had been able to maintain its level of employment then operating profits would have grown at an annual average rate of 4.2 per cent over the period, rather than at an average of 1.4 per cent.

In addition, the strong growth of wages per head relative to the growth of the productivity substantially reduced the growth of operating profits. If wages had grown at 3 per cent per annum instead of 5 per cent, then operating profits would have increased on average by 5 per cent each year. In this case, it would appear that the firm could have reduced the growth of wages without having a significant impact upon employment and productivity growth.

4.6 CONCLUSIONS

The basic premise underlying this chapter is that attention to, and analysis of, the processes within the modern corporation which generate sustained long-run growth of productivity is essential in understanding firm performance and in evaluating alternative strategies for the firm. It is the theory of complex, self-organising institutions which directs us towards the corporate culture of the enterprise and the extent to which this allows learning processes to flourish and to dictate the future evolution of the company. The model we have developed seeks to enumerate these processes and the corporate culture in general in terms of the coefficient reflecting the long-run growth of productivity within the firm.

In this chapter we have shown how this information on productivity, together with a quantification of the long-term evolution of average wages and employment, can be used to classify firms. We suggest a delineation between firms whose growth of overall operating profits is driven primarily by strong technological performance and those where selling and marketing are the dominant forces behind profit growth. In general, we argue that in the short to medium term firms are constrained by their corporate culture, as reflected in the trend rate of growth of productivity. This view tends to be confirmed by the tendency for the most productive and profitable firms, particularly in the mature chemicals and pharmaceuticals sector, to show faster growth of profits and productivity.

This approach to corporate growth stresses the importance of the quality and motivation of the individual to the nature of interactions within the firm, and so to the learning processes which dictate the evolution of the enterprise. In this chapter we have demonstrated the positive relationship between the trend growth of productivity and the trend growth of wages per individual. Clearly the returns to workers are related to their productivity but this relationship also suggests that firms which constrain wage growth substantially below the growth of productivity will have difficulty maintaining such productivity growth in the long term, since it will become increasingly difficult to attract and retain the best personnel. On the other hand, firms which allow trend wage growth to approach or exceed the trend growth of productivity will also find it difficult to sustain productivity growth. Investment in R&D, the other key factor behind productivity growth together with learning processes, will be constrained. In Chapter 5 we turn to discuss how the model developed here can be used to assess the performance of firms involved in mergers.

Finally, the chapter has shown how the model, and the focus upon the trend in the growth of productivity, profitability, wages and employment, can be helpful in appraising different business plans and perspectives. An important conclusion from the analysis of restructuring is that short-term changes in employment tend not to be compensated by increases in the trend rate of growth of productivity which, as we have argued, is determined by the long-run learning processes and corporate culture of the firm. This entails that restructuring which leads to a significant decline in employment will tend to depress the rate of growth of profits.

5 Quantitative Analysis of Mergers

5.1 INTRODUCTION

In addition to internal growth processes firms also have the opportunity to increase their size through mergers. Indeed, during certain periods this has been a very popular means of expansion leading to an increasing concentration of activity amongst a declining number of firms. However, previous studies suggest that the impact of mergers on firm performance is not generally clear. There is still much debate as to what are the conditions that are necessary for a merger to be successful in the long run.

Here we argue that a crucial factor in the long-term success of a merger is the extent to which the *corporate cultures of the combining firms are compatible*. This is important in determining how, and how far, the combined firm is able to evolve and develop in its new environment. Here again, what matters are the learning and innovative processes within the enlarged firm which determine how the firm defines, and responds to, the problems that it faces. We suggest that this can be assessed using the model of productivity growth by looking at the relative trend growth of productivity and of profit growth of the two firms prior to the merger. The model also allows us to present some scenarios for the merged firm in the years following the merger.

We simulate the value of productivity for the merged firm in the years after the merger by taking the weighted average of the value of the trend of the value added per head of the two firms in the year before the merger and then apply to this the weighted average value of the growth coefficient of the two firms. The same calculation is also made for the development of wages and salaries. As far as the number of employees is concerned, we simply add the numbers employed by the two firms. This allows us to calculate the trend in operating profit per head for the merged firm and the resulting movement in overall operating profit. The weights are given by the employment share of each firm in the total combined employment of the two companies in the year before the merger (see Box 5.1, p. 79, for a technical description of the approach that is adopted).

Box 5.1   Predicting post-merger trends

The formula used to estimate the resulting trend in the productivity of the merged firm in the years of the merger is the following:

$$MA_f^{1+2} = MA_{tf-1}^1 * \frac{pN_{tf-1}^1}{pN_{tf-1}^1 + pN_{tf-1}^2} + MA_{tf-1}^2 * \frac{pN_{tf-1}^2}{pN_{tf-1}^1 + pN_{tf-1}^2}$$

$$kal_f^{1+2} = kal_{tf-1}^1 * \frac{pN_{tf-1}^1}{pN_{tf-1}^1 + pN_{tf-1}^2} + kal_{tf-1}^2 * \frac{pN_{tf-1}^2}{pN_{tf-1}^1 + pN_{tf-1}^2}$$

The predicted value of productivity of the merged firm is thus given by the value of the trend in value added per head of firm 1 in the year before the merger (MA_{tf-1}^1) multiplied by the employment of firm 1 (pN_{tf-1}^1) divided by the total number of employees of the two firms plus the value of the trend value added per head of firm 2 in the year prior to the merger multiplied by the employment share of firm 2. In short, the value of productivity of the merged firm is predicted as a weighted average of the trend in value added of the two firms prior to the merger with the weights being given by the share of overall employment accounted for by each of the firms.

In a second step, this value is increased by the average weighted growth coefficient (k_{al}) with the weights again being given by the pre-merger employment share:

per cent of employment of firm 1 = Employment of firm 1/ (Employment of firm 1+ Employment of firm 2)

So, to be able to make this type of analysis data needs to be available to determine the growth coefficient or trend of the productivity and the wages and salaries of the two firms over a sufficient period before the merger takes place. We proceed by looking at a number of actual mergers where data are available to us which permits the computation of the trend values of productivity, profit and employment growth prior to the merger. In these cases we are able to define only the trend in growth for the two merging companies before they merge and then plot the predicted trend evolution for the merged firm. In the first case which we discuss below we are able to compare the predicted outcome from the model with the observed outcome for the firm in the year of the merger. In the other cases the merger took place in 2000 and we have no post-merger data.

Later in the chapter we discuss two cases where we can identify the trend in growth prior to the merger and also, but more tentatively, we look at the trend rate of growth of productivity for the merged firm. However, in these cases we have data only to identify the pre-merger trend for one, the dominant, of the merging firms. We start with an analysis of the merger between two electronics companies, Compaq and DEC.

5.2   MERGER OF COMPAQ AND DEC (DIGITAL EQUIPMENT COMPANY), 1998

Table 5.1 presents summary data for Compaq and DEC prior to their merger, together with the predicted value for the main variables in the year of the merger. This information shows DEC to be the much larger partner in the merger in terms of employment, with roughly two-thirds of the combined personnel of the two firms being employed by DEC. In terms of productivity, however, employees in Compaq generated almost twice as much value added per person than their counterparts in DEC. The size of DEC in terms of employment ensures that the predicted level of average value added per head for the merged firm in the year of the merger is considerably below that of Compaq.

Table 5.1   Summary features of Compaq and DEC merger

Deflated trend value	Compaq (1997)	DEC (1997)	Predicted value in merger year (1998)	Actual Value (1998)
Employment (number)	32 565	54 900		62 565
Value added per head (000$)	130	54	94	35.9
Wages per head (000$)	69	44	59	55
Operating profit per head (000$)	61	10	35	−19
Market value[1]	8.9	9.5		19

Note: [1]   Market value = Market capitalisation/Operating profit (see Chapter 6, p. 95, for a more detailed discussion of this measure).

Table 5.1 also shows that the high productivity in Compaq was associated with high wages per head relative to those paid in DEC. This points to problems that the merged firm could face in reconciling the different productivity and wage structures of the two component firms. In terms of operating profit, employees in Compaq were able to generate almost five times more profit per person than their counterparts in DEC.

The final two columns of the table show the predicted values for these variables for the merged firm obtained by using the average values of the trend growth coefficients of the two firms prior to the merger, together with the actual outcome in the year of the merger. This is obviously a very preliminary assessment and so the analysis should be treated very cautiously. Both employment and operating profit per head fell substantially in the year of the merger, with the result that overall operating profits slumped. Actual productivity, too, was much lower than the extension of the average of the pre-merger trends would suggest, while average wages were much closer to that predicted by the model. The final row of the table shows the market value of the two firms prior to the merger and the market value of the combined firm in 1998, the year of the merger.

We proceed to consider the calibrated growth coefficients of the two firms during the 10-year period prior to their merger, and briefly discuss some implications for the merged firm. Table 5.2 presents these growth coefficients for each firm, together with the weighted average coefficient for the merged firm.

Although the level of productivity in Compaq was considerably higher than that of DEC prior to the merger, as was shown in Table 5.1, here we see that the trend rate of growth of value added in DEC, over the decade before the merger, was a little higher. The trend rate of growth of value added for DEC was 3.1 per cent while that for Compaq was 2.6 per cent (see also Figure 5.1). However, the trend rate

Table 5.2   Growth coefficients for Compaq and DEC merger

	Compaq (%)	DEC (%)	Merger year (%)
Growth of value added per head	2.6	3.1	2.8
Growth of average wage	2.5	7	5
Growth of operating profit per head	3	−5	−1
Employment growth	19	−10	4.5
Growth of operating profits	22	−15	3.5

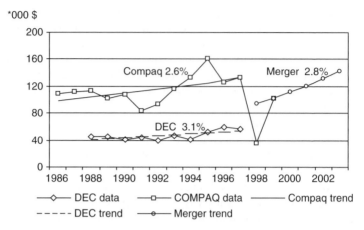

Figure 5.1   Growth of (deflated) value added per head for Compaq and DEC, 1986–2002

of growth of wages and salaries for DEC was much higher than the rate of growth of value-added (see Figure 5.3). There was a negative trend rate of employment growth for DEC of 10 per cent per year, but this was not sufficient to prevent a considerable trend decline in operating profit per head and in total operating profits (Figures 5.2 and 5.4). Thus, although DEC exhibited a relatively strong techno-logical performance, in terms of the growth of value added per person, the trends in wages and profits were not sustainable.

Compaq, on the other hand, exhibited slower productivity growth but much more limited growth of wages and salaries and therefore a modest but positive increase in operating profit per head. Compaq, however, was able to expand employment at a substantial rate over the 10-year period, suggesting considerable proficiency in marketing and sales. This combination of a modest increase in productivity and wages together with rapid growth of employment led to a large trend increase in overall operating profits.

Figures 5.1–5.4 plot the actual and the calibrated trend values for productivity, operating profit and wages and salaries for each firm together with the predicted values in the immediate post-merger period. The graphs demonstrate the higher level but slower growth of produc-tivity and wages in salaries for Compaq relative to DEC in the years before the merger and the predicted trend values after 1998 when the merger took place. The merger appears to have induced a strong

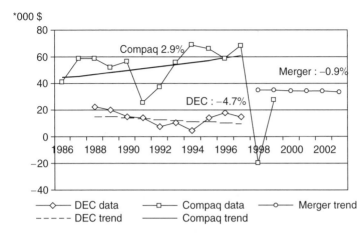

Figure 5.2   Growth of operating profit per head for Compaq and DEC, 1986–2002

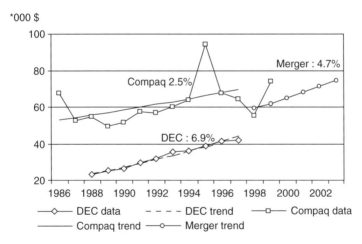

Figure 5.3   Growth of wages per head for Compaq and DEC, 1986–2002

decrease in productivity as well as in operating profit per head for the merged firm which is much stronger than that calculated by the weighted average value of the trend of the value added per head of the two firms for the year prior to the merger and the weighted average value of its growth coefficient.

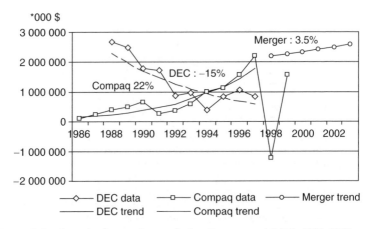

Figure 5.4   Growth of operating profit for Compaq and DEC, 1986–2002

It is also interesting to note that this analysis highlights differences in the way that actual productivity and profits vary about the estimated trend for the two firms. Looking at Figure 5.1 suggests that these two firms are affected differently by the economic cycle in terms of both the extent of volatility and the timing of the upturns and downturns in productivity and operating profits per head.

5.3   MERGER OF PFIZER AND WARNER-LAMBERT, 2000

We now present a similar analysis of the merger between two pharmaceuticals companies, Pfizer and Warner-Lambert, that took place in 2000. Here we have no post-merger information with which to compare our predicted values for the combined company. This example is interesting since the two companies exhibited very similar characteristics prior to the merger in terms of technological and marketing and sales performance. Table 5.3 shows the trend values of employment, value added per head, wages and operating profit per head in the final year before the merger and the predicted values for the merged firm. In this case, the combined amount of employment was more evenly distributed between the two firms, with Pfizer accounting for 54 per cent of the total prior to the merger. Pfizer exhibited a higher level of value added per head than Warner-Lambert, although the difference was only around 20 per cent. In the Compaq and DEC case analysed above the pre-merger difference in average individual productivity levels between the two firms was over 50 per cent. The level of wages per head for Pfizer and Warner-Lambert were also very similar, while Pfizer was able to generate 33 per cent more operating profit per head than Warner-Lambert.

In terms of the trend performance over the previous decade and more, the growth coefficient for value added per head was slightly higher for Warner-Lambert than for Pfizer. The trend in the other variables – wages and salaries, operating profit per head, employment and overall operating profit – were very similar for both companies.

Figures 5.5–5.7 demonstrate that for Warner-Lambert there was a slightly lower level of productivity, operating profit per head, wages per head and overall operating profit compared with Pfizer. However, the trend growth in these variables is very similar for the two firms. It is also noticeable that, particularly in the early 1990s, these two firms responded in very similar ways to the economic cycle. The pattern of variation about the estimated trend line is very similar for the two firms.

Table 5.3 Summary features of Pfizer and Warner-Lambert merger

	Pfizer	Warner-Lambert	Merger year
Employment (%)	54	46	
Value added per head (000$)	142	111	135
Wages per head (000$)	87	74.3	84
Operating profit per head (000$)	55	36.7	51

Table 5.4 Growth coefficients for Pfizer and Warner-Lambert merger

	Pfizer (%)	Warner-Lambert (%)	Merger year (%)
Growth of value added per head	5.9	5.6	5.75
Growth of wages per head	4.4	4.3	4.4
Growth of operating profit per head	8.4	9.5	8.9
Growth of employment	3.1	2.5	2.8
Growth of operating profit	11.5	12.1	11.8

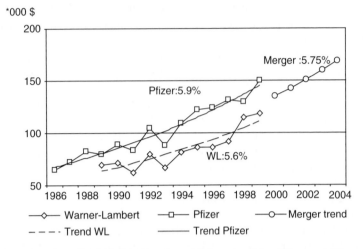

Figure 5.5   Growth of (deflated) value added per head for Pfizer and Warner-Lambert, 1986–2004

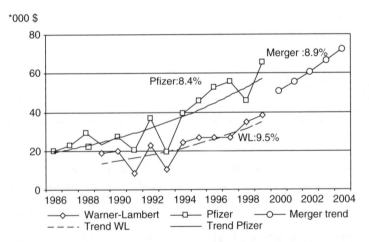

Figure 5.6   Growth of operating profit per head for Pfizer and Warner-Lambert, 1986–2004

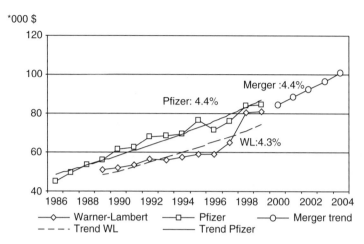

Figure 5.7 Growth of wages per head for Pfizer and Warner-Lambert, 1986–2004

5.4 MERGER OF DOW AND UNION CARBIDE, 2000

The merger of DOW and Union Carbide (UC) provides an example of a large firm merging with a smaller firm, in terms of employment, where the current values of productivity and operating profit per head are similar but the trends over the previous 13 or so years for some of the variables are different. DOW employed more than twice as many employees as Union Carbide in the year before their merger (Table 5.5). Nevertheless, productivity levels in that year were very similar with value added per head in Union Carbide being around 97 per cent of the level of DOW. The level of operating profit per head was also very similar in the year prior to the merger with that of Union Carbide being 8 per cent higher than that of DOW. A more significant difference is apparent for levels of employee remuneration where the average wage at Union Carbide was only two-thirds of that of DOW.[1]

Table 5.6 and Figures 5.8–5.10 show the trend performance of the two firms. Trend growth of value added per head for Union Carbide has been slightly higher than that of DOW, although both companies exhibit considerable variability around the computed trend value. On the other hand, the trend growth of average wages has been positive for

DOW but negative for Union Carbide. There was a large increase in average wages at DOW in the mid-1990s followed by an even large downward correction which brought wage levels back towards those of Union Carbide.

The fact that trend productivity growth was similar for the two firms but the growth of wages was divergent is reflected in the slightly different trend in the growth of operating profit. The trend growth of operating profits at Union Carbide was higher than that of DOW, although again there is considerable volatility around the trend. The employment trend for both firms has been negative, but more pronounced for Union Carbide, so that the growth of overall operating profits has been less than that of profit per head.

Here again the data in Figures 5.8–5.10 demonstrate a very high degree of similarity in the time profile of the variation in productivity and operating profits per head for the two firms. Both firms seem to be more susceptible to changes in economic conditions than the firms previously analysed in this chapter, but the pattern of changes in productivity and profits are almost identical for the two firms. Hence we may conclude that they are affected by the business cycle in the same way.

Table 5.5   Summary features of DOW and Union Carbide (UC) merger

	DOW	UC	Merger year
Employment (%)	77	23	
Value added per head (*000$)	97.4	94	99
Wages per head (*000$)	28.7	19.2	30.7
Operating profit per head (*000$)	68.7	74.8	68.3

Table 5.6   Growth coefficients for DOW and Union Carbide merger

	DOW (%)	UC (%)	Merger year (%)
Growth of value added per head	2.7	3.5	3
Growth of wages per head	3.5	−1.2	2.4
Growth of operating profit per head	2.4	6	3.2
Growth of employment	−3.2	−3.6	−4.8
Growth of overall operating profit	−0.8	1.2	−0.4

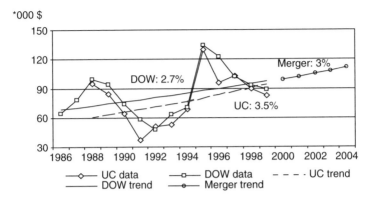

Figure 5.8   Growth of (deflated) value added per head for DOW and Union Carbide, 1986–2004

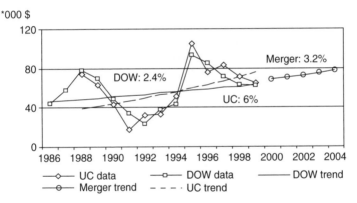

Figure 5.9   Growth of operating profit per head for DOW and Union Carbide, 1986–2004

5.5   ANALYSIS OF HISTORICAL MERGERS

We now look at two mergers that took place in the more distant past, which allow us to provide some analysis of the post-merger performance of the combined firm. We are not able to simulate the impact of the merger since we do have sufficient data for both of the firms prior to the merger taking place, so we have looked at the main trends for the dominant firm in the merger. We consider American Home Products

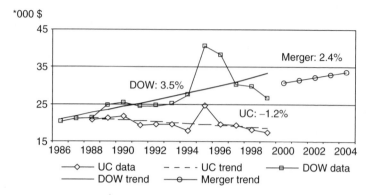

Figure 5.10   Growth of wages per head for Dow and Union Carbide, 1986–2004

(AHP), which bought American Cyanamid Corporation in 1994, and Merck, which purchased a number of firms in 1993.

Our analysis allows us to compute the trend growth of productivity for the dominant firm in the 10 years before the merger and the subsequent growth rate of value added per head in the years after the merger. Figure 5.11 shows that productivity in Merck was growing at a very fast rate, over 9 per cent, in the years before the merger activity, but that this rate of productivity growth declined for the post-merger firm to less than 5 per cent. The graph also shows that the absolute value of productivity of the enlarged firm fell sharply in the year of the merger but increased greatly in the next year. In the second year after the merger the pre-merger level of productivity had been re-attained. Subsequent growth was then more muted than for the pre-merger firm.

The figure for AHP, Figure 5.12, also shows a strong negative impact on value added per head in the year of the merger and then a subsequent rapid increase such that the level of productivity of the merged firm was considerably higher than that of the pre-merger firm. However, again the trend rate of productivity growth after these initial adjustments appears to have been slower for the merged firm. The development of employment also differs notably for these two cases. In both cases, as one would expect, there was a significant increase in employment in the year of the merger, and a subsequent rationalisa-tion of employees. However, in the case of Merck, as shown in Figure 5.13, the trend rate of growth of employment of the pre-merger firm

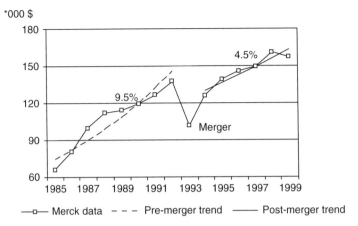

Figure 5.11 Growth of value added per head for Merck, before and after merger, 1985–99

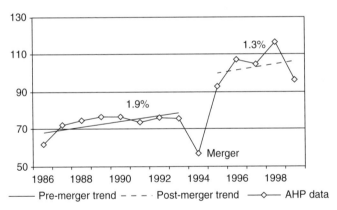

Figure 5.12 Growth of value added per head for AHP, before and after merger, 1986–98

was maintained. In the case of AHP, where the proportional change in employment in the merger year was much greater than that for Merck (Figure 5.14), the trend in employment for the merged firm was negative with the pre-merger level of employment having been reached within about 5 years.

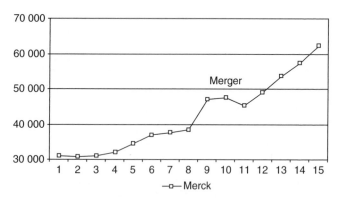

Figure 5.13   Growth of employment for Merck, before and after merger

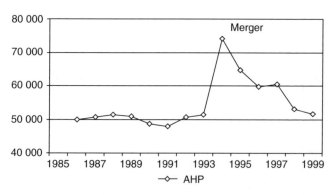

Figure 5.14   Growth of employment for AHP, before and merger, 1985–99

5.6   CONCLUSIONS

In this chapter we have applied our model of the growth of companies to assess the performance of firms involved in selected mergers. The objective has been to show how the model can be used to define the key features of firms involved in mergers and how this may be of use in assessing the prospects of the merged firm, while we have avoided making any judgements ourselves.

The approach of this book to the growth of the firm suggests that the principal factor determining the long-run growth of the firm is the corporate culture of the enterprise and the extent to which this allows and stimulates learning processes. In this context, this chapter suggests that the long-run success of a merger will depend upon the extent to which learning processes and corporate culture are enhanced or under-mined in the merged firm. This will determine whether the long-run growth processes exhibited by the firms prior to their merger are strengthened or weakened. We will show in Chapter 6 that the market value of a firm is strongly related to the trend growth of profitability. Thus, in the long run, the market value of the merged firm will reflect the extent to which the merger raises the trend rate of growth of productivity of the new firm.

6 Application of the Model as an Investment Tool

6.1 INTRODUCTION

In Chapter 4 we provided an analysis of firm performance from an internal point of view and discussed the application of the approach to modelling corporate productivity growth as a tool for management. Here we discuss how the ideas concerning the nature of the firm and the way that it evolves and the model which reflects these can be used as an analytical tool from an external point of view, and specifically in terms of informing long-term portfolio investment choices. Our focus is entirely upon long-run investment decisions. This follows from the view of the firm as a complex self-organising institution which, because of increasing returns and positive feedback effects from learning and experience, tends to exhibit a sustained and constant process of growth. Deviations around this trend rate of growth tend to be associated with the business cycle. As we have argued earlier, in the medium term, firms are generally bound by their trend rate of growth of productivity.

In general the theory of complex, self-organising institutions, as applied here to modern corporations, suggests that those companies with a corporate culture which stimulates and exploits the learning capacities and experience of its employees will tend to exhibit stronger growth of productive potential. We believe that our analysis, by identifying firms with strong trend growth performance and hence an effective corporate culture, therefore provides a means of selecting firms which are likely to generate the strongest returns in the long-run. This follows from the propositions that growth of productivity and growth of operating profit per head are correlated and that, in turn, as we shall show, the trend in the growth of profits is strongly related to the market valuation of a company. Our method also provides a means of assessing the degree of risk associated with the predicted growth rate of a particular company, in terms of the strength of the estimate of the growth coefficient. The accuracy of the estimated trend rate of growth tends to be lower for firms that seem particularly susceptible to the business cycle. We should stress here that this approach is not of relevance for short-term speculative investments.

The chapter starts by providing a general analysis, of interest to both investors and managers, showing how the trend rate of growth of operating profit is strongly related to a measure of the market valuation of the firm. This implies that firms that grow strongly in the future, in terms of productivity and profitability, will tend to have higher market valuation. In addition, the analysis is able to identify firms that deviate substantially from the estimated relationship between growth performance and market value. For firms where the market value exceeds that suggested by the trend in the growth of profits, it is possible that in the longer term the market value of this firm will be revised downwards relative to that of other firms in the sector. On the other hand, firms that are currently undervalued relative to their growth performance can be expected to be re-valued upwards by the market over the longer term. This may be useful information for portfolio investors. It may also be helpful to management since undervalued firms may well be the targets for acquisition by other firms.

6.2   THE RELATION BETWEEN THE TREND GROWTH OF OPERATING PROFITS AND MARKET VALUE

We start by discussing Figure 6.1 for the chemicals and pharmaceuticals companies and Figure 6.2 for the electronics firms, showing the relationship between the trend growth in operating profit, as generated from applying a simple exponential regression approach to actual data for firms over a 10-year period or more, and data on the market value of the firm. Our measure of market value is very similar to that used by financial analysts and is derived from the ratio of the sum of market capitalisation[1] and the sum of operating profits over the 10-year period. This ratio corresponds to a trend value of the price earnings ratio.

Figures 6.1 and 6.2 both demonstrate a strong positive relationship between the trend growth of operating profits and the market value of the firm.[2] Firms that exhibit a strong trend rate of growth of profitability also tend to be valued highly by the market. The estimated relationship is quite strong for both sectors. The correlation coefficients, R^2, which are shown on the graphs, are a statistical measure of the strength of the relationship between the trend rate of growth of profits and market value. A value of one would suggest that market value is perfectly explained by the trend in profit growth. On the other

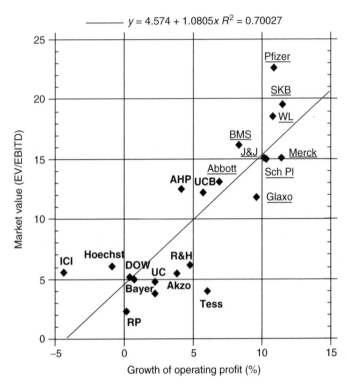

Figure 6.1   Correlation between trend growth of operating profit and market value for chemicals and pharmaceuticals firms

hand, a value close to zero would imply that profit growth has little relationship with market value. In these particular cases, the correlation coefficients are high and show that for the chemicals and pharmaceuticals sector around 70 per cent of the variation in market value across these firms can be explained by the trend in their growth performance. For the electronics firms the correlation is even stronger, with about 89 per cent of the variation in market value being explained by growth performance. Thus, in general, the magnitude of the trend rate of growth of profits is a good predictor of market value. This regression approach provides an estimate of the relationship on average between profit growth and market value. There are, however, instances where for particular firms there is a substantial deviation between their performance and the average relationship for the sector. Firms that lie substantially above the estimated line, such as Pfizer,

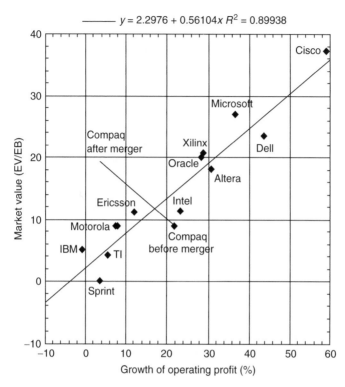

Figure 6.2   Correlation between trend growth of operating profit and market value for electronics firms

have been, on average, overvalued by the market relative to the performance of the firm in terms of the trend in the growth of profits. On the other hand, firms, such as Dell, which are located below the estimated regression line have been, on average, undervalued by the market relative to the trend in the growth of profits.

This analysis thus demonstrates that those firms within a sector which generate the strongest trend growth of profits tend to be those firms which are most highly valued by the market. This implies that within a sector firms with the best growth performance will offer the greatest prospect for a relatively strong increase in the market valuation of the enterprise. From a managerial point of view, if the corporate culture of the enterprise is weak relative to that of other firms in the sector then it will prove difficult to generate rapidly rising productivity and profits over the medium to long term. This will tend to be reflected in a relatively low market value, which may make the firm vulnerable to acquisition by another firm which believes that it can instil a superior corporate culture and so generate stronger profit growth.

It is important to note here that, as we have discussed before, growth of profits reflects two underlying factors, the trend in the growth of operating profit per head and the number of employees. The trend in operating profit per head is closely related to the long-run growth in productivity, which reflects the strength of learning effects and research efforts and the quality of the corporate culture. These are long-run processes within the firm.

The trend in the number of employees, on the other hand, is subject to alteration following a change in market conditions. For the electronics firms market conditions have been such that a consistent long-term trend in employment can be discerned for most firms. A similar situation is apparent for pharmaceuticals companies. However, as we discussed earlier, for chemicals firms the trend in the number of employees changed at the end of the 1980s from moderately increasing to more strongly decreasing in the 1990s. This is reflected in the lower trend rate of profit growth for these firms. Firms which shed jobs at a rate faster than the trend increase in productivity will not be able to generate increasing operating profits unless they constrain the growth of wages and salaries. As we showed in Chapter 4, this would have implications for the future growth of productivity.

6.3   THE CORRELATION BETWEEN THE RETURN ON INVESTMENT AND MARKET VALUE

We now complement this analysis of the relationship between the trend growth of profitability and market value with an examination of the correlation between market value and another measure of firm performance; the return on invested capital (ROIC). Analysts, such as Goldman Sachs, use the latter measure in their reports on sectors such as pharmaceuticals.[3] Here our measure of market value is adjusted slightly as market capitalisation relative to the sum of invested capital, where invested capital includes the capitalisation of expenditures on R&D. Owing to lack of reliable investment data we approximate invested capital as

Invested capital = (Value added + R&D) / Sales

ROIC is given by the sum of profits over the relevant 10-year period divided by the sum of invested capital over the same number of years.

Figures 6.3 and 6.4 show the estimated relationship between ROIC and market value for chemicals and pharmaceuticals firms and electronics firms, respectively. These graphs suggest a relatively strong correlation between ROIC and market value for the chemicals and pharmaceuticals firms and a slightly weaker relationship for the electronics firms. Interestingly our results for the pharmaceuticals firms are similar to, but stronger than, those of Goldman Sachs.

Figures 6.3 and 6.4 give an additional complementary view of the relationship between the long-run performance of the firm and the value placed upon the firm by the market. Again, for firms which are

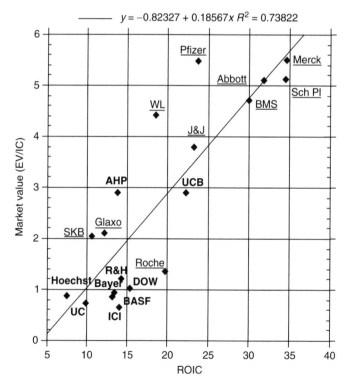

Figure 6.3   Correlation between return on investment and market value for chemicals and pharmaceuticals firms

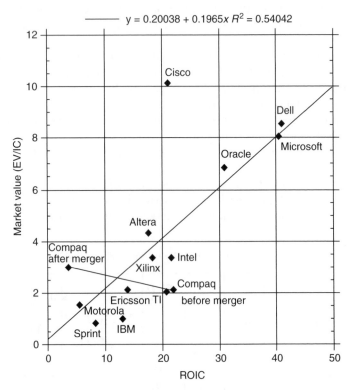

Figure 6.4   Correlation between the return on investment and market value for electronics firms

located substantially away from the estimated regression line, the market value of the firm in relation to the computed value for ROIC deviates from the average relationship suggested for the sector as a whole. One can conclude that for firms that lie substantially above the line, the market value exceeds the value that would be consistent with the observed ROIC. This implies either that there are reasons to expect that ROIC for the firm will increase, and that this is being reflected in the market value or, if there are no such reasons, that the firm is overvalued. Similarly, for firms substantially below the regression line there may be grounds to believe that ROIC will fall or, if not, then the firm would appear to be undervalued by the market.

6.4   SELECTING COMPANIES FOR A LONG-RUN INVESTMENT PORTFOLIO

Given the above analysis of the relation between the trend in the growth of operating profits and the market value of a firm, we now proceed to discuss how the output from the model may be of use in informing portfolio investment decisions where the investor is looking for returns over the longer run. The essence of our approach derives from the view of the firm as a self-organising institution that is far from equilibrium, whereby internal processes within the firm act so as to generate sustained and constant growth of productivity in the medium to long term. The strength of the coefficient of growth that is observed in the past, which reflects the nature of the corporate culture of the enterprise, therefore provides an indicator of the potential magnitude of future growth.

The model allows an identification of those firms where productivity is likely to grow faster than the average. This information can then be combined with an analysis of the trend in the growth of employees to categorise firms as more 'market oriented' or 'technologically oriented'. In general, we conclude that the latter are more likely to generate sustained increases in profits. This information on the trend rate of growth of productivity and profitability can, and should, be supplemented by a measure of the reliability of the estimated growth coefficient. The essence of our approach is to identify the trend rate of growth from observations over at least a 10-year period. In general, the greater the variability of the data around the estimated trend line the less reliable is the estimated trend. In other words, the more sensitive a company to the business cycle, and so the greater the variability in that company's output and profitability, the more difficult it is accurately to isolate the trend from cyclical movements. The statistical measure of the extent to which the estimated trend explains the observed variation in the data for the firm is the correlation coefficient, represented by R^2. A relatively high value of R^2 suggests that the fitted exponential curve will continue to be a reliable indicator of the trend in the future and also that future growth will be less prone to cyclical movements in the market. Hence, on this basis, the long-term choice of firms for an investment portfolio can be based upon the magnitude of the trend coefficient and the strength of the relationship between the trend and the data.

In Table 6.1 we show the estimated trend coefficients and associated R^2 for a selection of companies from the chemicals and pharmaceuticals sector and the electronics industry. An approach that could be applied to selecting firms for an investment portfolio might start by excluding from the analysis firms with a statistically weak estimated trend growth of operating profits. A general rule could be to exclude firms with a value of R^2 of less than, say, 0.7. A choice could then be made between the remaining firms, for each sector, on the basis of the magnitude of the estimated growth coefficient. Finally, this information could be supplemented by a classification of firms according to whether recent growth of operating profits has been driven mainly by technological performance – that is, the growth of productivity – or by success in the market, where selling and marketing performance have been the driving force.

Finally, in Figure 6.5 we show how the modelling approach can be used in the simple choice between investment in two firms, *A* and *B*, operating in the same market. In this case, the application of the model provides unambiguous information. The trend growth of profitability for Firm *A* is greater than that of Firm *B* *and* our confidence in the estimated value of the growth coefficient, as reflected

Table 6.1   Growth and correlation coefficients for selected firms

Firm	Trend rate of growth of operating profit	Correlation coefficient R^2
A Chemicals and pharmaceuticals companies		
AHP	5.3	0.63
J&J	9.9	0.95
Merck	12.2	0.97
Pfizer	11.5	0.78
Abbott	7	0.97
BMS	8.6	0.69
WL	12.1	0.57
Sch Pl	11.5	0.98
Glaxo	10.9	0.89
B Electronics companies		
Microsoft	33.8	0.99
Intel	29.8	0.94
TI	8.13	0.62
Sprint	3.5	0.45
Dell	46.6	0.93
Oracle	29.11	0.94
Altera	31.6	0.88
Xilinx	29.2	0.91

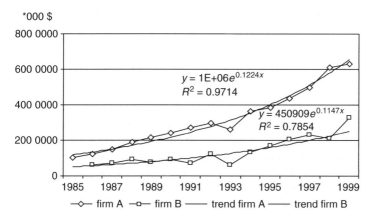

Figure 6.5   Trend growth of (deflated) operating profit for two pharmaceuticals firms, 1985–99

by the value of R^2, is higher for A than for B. For instance, where the growth coefficient is higher but the correlation coefficient is lower the individual is left with a choice between a higher value of predicted return but greater risk or lower risk together with a lower potential return.

When comparing a range of firms within a sector, we believe that our suggested approach of excluding firms with a computed correlation coefficient below a certain threshold level and then choosing firms with the highest trend growth coefficients will lead to a portfolio which exhibits above-average returns in the longer term with a moderate degree of risk. This approach is therefore not of use for those seeking high returns but with a high degree of risk.

6.5   CONCLUSIONS

In this chapter we have suggested that an understanding of the processes which generate growth of productivity and profitability in modern corporations can be useful in identifying firms which are currently under valued or overvalued by the market in relation to their past trend performance. In addition, given that these processes are fundamentally determined by the corporate culture of the enterprise, we expect that firms which exhibit a strong corporate culture in their past performance, are more likely to produce good performance in the future.

It is important to stress that the assessment of past performance is derived from the analysis of the trend in productivity and profitability over a medium-term period of at least 10 years. Because all firms, to varying degrees, are susceptible to cyclical fluctuations of the economy, projections based upon only a few years of data will be less reliable. Our approach, we believe, gets closer to the essential and fundamental factors that underlie the long-run process of corporate growth. The contention of this chapter is that a better understanding of this process, and its numerical reflection in the estimated growth coefficients, provides useful information when assessing the current market value of a company and the potential for that valuation to increase over time relative to the valuation of other companies competing in the same sector.

7 Conclusions

7.1 GENERAL OBSERVATIONS

The main message which this book seeks to convey is a simple, and perhaps obvious, one, that an important part of analysis of the performance of modern corporations, from the perspective of both managers and investors, should be attention to the *processes* generating long-run growth of productivity and profits. We have sought to provide a theoretical background to this view and a simple empirical model which identifies a representation of these processes in terms of coefficients measuring the trend evolution of the main strategic variables for the firm.

The theoretical justification for this is based upon the view of the multi-product firm as a complex, self-organising institution which survives and evolves far from any concept of equilibrium. The firm is a dynamic body which is regularly changing its structure and internal organisation and generating new possibilities and opportunities. The corporation is an association of individuals, and their ideas, which is constantly seeking ways to improve and extend the activities that are undertaken.

Firms operate in a chaotic and unpredictable environment. Nevertheless, the analysis of complexity suggests that the nature of self-organisation generates order out of chaos. The processes that characterise self-organising firms far from equilibrium tend to be irreversible so that increasing returns and positive feedback effects are important, resulting in a process of self-reinforcing growth for the firm. So, despite the range of possible outcomes that are feasible in such an uncertain environment, self-organising firms tend to perform in regular and predictable ways. From this, an understanding of past behaviour can be used to make future projections of the growth of the firm and to identify those firms within a sector which offer the prospects for strongest growth.

We have argued that the factor that determines the magnitude of the growth processes that result from the natural tendencies of the self-organising firm is the corporate culture of the enterprise. 'Corporate culture' comprises a range of factors determining the way that the firm responds, adjusts and evolves. Of most importance are the quality of the individual employees, in terms of their education, training and motivation, and how the stock of knowledge and experience embodied in the employees as a whole is utilised within the firm. Corporate culture is fundamental in determining how the benefits of R&D, together with learning and experience, are translated into the growth of productivity of the firm.

Our empirical application data for actual companies facilitates a numerical assessment of differences in corporate culture across companies, in terms of the extent to which opportunities from R&D and from experience are actually translated into higher productivity and higher profits. Following on from this, we argue that in the medium term firms are constrained by their corporate culture, so that estimated trends in the growth of productivity and profits, based upon sufficient observations, are likely to provide useful indicators of future developments. In other words, firms will tend to be bound by the factors which determine the strength of growth processes, and these factors, which comprise corporate culture, cannot be quickly and easily changed. We believe that the correlation between the market value of firms and the trend growth of operating profit, as shown in Chapter 6, provides a confirmation of the importance of the processes generating trend growth of the firm which we have sought to identify in our empirical work.

7.2 BROAD IMPLICATIONS FOR MANAGEMENT

This view has important implications for management. At a general level

for an organisation to seek stable equilibrium relationships with an environment which is inherently unpredictable is bound to lead to failure. Successful strategies, especially in the longer term, do not result from fixing an organisational intention and mobilising around it; they emerge from complex and continuing interactions between people.[1]

Similarly, the complexity approach shows that 'for an entity to survive and thrive it needs to explore its space of possibilities and to encourage variety...the search for a single "optimum" strategy is neither possible nor desirable'.[2] Success may stem more from allowing self-reinforcing processes to operate than from specific interventions to achieve a particular vision.

A key consideration for management is how to foster learning, which is central to the process of endogenous change within the organisation. The aim should be to create an infrastructure which enables experimentation and the development of new ideas so as to create different patterns of relationships, new structures within the firm and innovative ways of working, which provide for more effective solutions to the problems that are faced. It is only by providing a *framework in which learning and adaptation can flourish* that companies with poor growth performance can hope to improve corporate culture.

The theories of complexity that underlie the approach of this book stress the importance of relationships and the institutional structure in which they develop. Complex adaptive social systems, such as firms, comprise networks of personal relationships, where the dynamics of the system are driven by interactions between individuals. 'How people relate to one another affects what emerges in the organisation – the culture, the creativity, the productivity.'[3] Management should provide the conditions under which creativity and innovativeness arise naturally within the company.

The basic view underlying these propositions is that for the complex self-organising firm that is far from equilibrium, it is more effective to allow solutions to problems to be defined by the people closest to the issue rather than to impose solutions from higher up. Complexity theorists, such as Stuart Kauffman,[4] argue that complex systems should not be controlled from above. If left alone it is clear that such systems do not become erratic and fall into chaos, but rather the process of self-organisation leads to the best solutions that could be achieved given the resources and nature of the firm. The outcome of this process is often a stable and orderly evolution of the firm. In essence, then, policies and decisions which enable these processes to work more effectively will lead to better outcomes for the firm than actions which interfere with or constrain the interactions between the individuals within the firm.

7.3 IMPLICATIONS FOR THE NATIONAL ECONOMY

If firms, as the major production units of the national economy, exhibit a tendency towards sustained and constant growth, then this feature should also be reflected in the growth performance of countries. It is to this issue that we finally and briefly turn. Indeed Figure 7.1 shows that a simple exponential approach to growth closely fits the

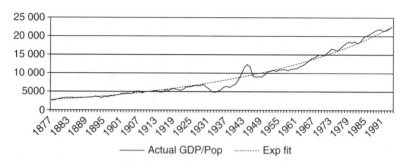

Figure 7.1   Actual productivity and the fit of the exponential growth model for the USA, 1877–1991

long-term evolution of national income per person in the USA. Similar figures can be obtained for a range of OECD countries.

In traditional economic theory growth is driven by the accumulation of capital, but with diminishing returns exogenously determined productivity growth is necessary to preserve the incentive to invest as output and the stock of capital increase. The approach to the firm developed in this book captures some of the key elements of the new growth theory, which states that consciously determined innovation, together with learning and rising skills' levels, will act to generate increasing returns and so sustain the incentive to invest at higher levels of income. The crucial processes which determine the growth of individual production units are thus relevant for understanding national productivity growth. In short, what is important is the amount of innovation which takes place in the economy and the way that new ideas and products, together with the accumulated experience in the economy as a whole, are utilised to raise productivity.

An important aspect of the development of the firm is interaction with the market. A similar relationship holds at the national level. The growth of productivity in the production of goods and services is influenced by the growth of consumption per person. We postulate here that the household is also an evolving adapting institution and the pace at which the household adjusts to new opportunities provided by new products constrains the rate at which productive capacity in the production sector of the economy can expand.

Finally, what does this short discussion imply for government policy? We have argued that for the individual complex, self-organising firm the best outcomes are likely to emerge in an environment which stimulates learning and the development of solutions to problems by those closest at hand. A framework needs to be in place to ensure that ideas and information are passed effectively to where they are needed in the firm, so that appropriate actions can be implemented. At the aggregate level, this also implies that the strongest growth processes will arise from unfettered interactions between individuals. The role for government is in ensuring that the general quality of the workforce, in terms of education, is rising and that there are appropriate incentives for firms to invest in R&D activities.

Notes

1 INTRODUCTION: MODERN ECONOMIC AND CORPORATE GROWTH

1. Kaldor (1961).
2. Kuznets (1966).
3. See, for example, Prigogine and Stengers (1997).
4. Arrow (1983).
5. Romer (1986).

2 ECONOMIC ANALYSIS OF GROWTH : A REVIEW

1. Penrose (1985).
2. Penrose (1959), p.1.
3. Solow (1956).
4. Arrow (1962).
5. See, for example, Romer (1986).
6. Romer (2000).
7. Grossman and Helpman (1993), p.122.
8. Schultz (1961), Becker (1993).
9. See, for example, Coleman (1988).
10. Penrose (1959).
11. 'Efficiency' is defined here in the narrow economic sense that there is no other allocation of resources that can make any one individual better off without making another individual worse off. This is known as a 'Pareto efficient allocation of resources'.
12. Penrose (1959), p.30.

3 MODELLING THE GROWTH OF CORPORATE PRODUCTIVITY

1. Schumpeter (1942).
2. Thaler (2000).
3. See also, Arthur (1994).
4. Thaler (2000).
5. See, for example, Arthur (1994).
6. Mitleton-Kelly (1998).
7. See, Prigogine and Stengers (1989).
8. See Guzzi and Sanglier (1997); Kauffman (1993).

9. Note the similarity here with the views of Penrose discussed in Chapter 2.
10. Arthur (1990).
11. Relevant work by the Boston Consulting Group is brought together in Stern and Stalk (1998).
12. Schmookler (1966).
13. Schmookler (1966) as quoted in Grossman and Helpman (1993).
14. This section is adapted from an earlier version published in *International Business Review*, vol 7: J. Solvay and M. Sanglier, 'A Model of the Growth of Corporate Productivity', 463–481, 1998, with permission from Elsevier Science.
15. The model was implemented with the package *ithink*.
16. All modern spreadsheets have the facility to perform this calculation.
17. The application of the model gives us the growth coefficient of EBITDA per head according to:

$$\frac{d(\text{EBITDA per head})}{dt} = \frac{\mathrm{d}}{dt}(MA) * salm - \frac{\mathrm{d}}{dt}(salm) * MA$$

where *MA* is value added per head and *salm* is the wage per head.

4   APPLICATION OF THE MODEL AS A MANAGEMENT TOOL

1. Nevertheless, a considerable amount of effort has been required to collect and process the information which is used in this and the following chapters.
2. Reflected in the model in the parameter k_{al}.
3. See the heavy dotted diagonal line in Figure 4.1.
4. Cases where the trend is not smooth, such as ICI, reflect the effects of currency conversion. The trend was calculated on data in the currency in which the annual reports are declared and then converted to a common currency for presentation.
5. The value of the term R^2 shows the extent to which the variation across firms of the growth of wages and salaries is explained by the observed values for the growth of productivity. A value of one would show that productivity growth for the firm explains perfectly the growth of wages and salaries. A value of zero would show no relationship at all.
6. This section is designed to give a quick indicative view of how the model of long-term productivity growth can be of use in assessing specific business plans. More details of how the approach can be used to assess a broader range of options can be obtained by contacting the authors via jacques.solvay@skynet.be, msanglier@ulb.ac.be, or paul.brenton@ceps.be.

5   QUANTITATIVE ANALYSIS OF MERGERS

1. The fact that the predicted values for the merged firm are, in some cases, greater than the values of the individual firms prior to the merger reflects

the similarity of the growth coefficients for the firms and the projection of the (weighted average) of these into the next period.

6 APPLICATION OF THE MODEL AS AN INVESTMENT TOOL

1. Market capitalisation is equal to the price of the share multiplied by the number of outstanding shares. Our measure differs slightly from that commonly used by excluding long-term debt. The rationale for this is that we are looking at the trend in long-term growth and market value and so neglect factors related to short-term changes in the economic environment and cyclical effects.
2. Note, however, the differences in the scales of the horizontal axes measuring the growth rate of profits so that the equations for the two sectors cannot be directly compared.
3. Goldman Sachs (2000).

7 CONCLUSIONS

1. Rosenhead (2000).
2. Mitleton-Kelly (1998).
3. Santosus (1998).
4. See Kauffman (1955).

Bibliography

ARROW, K. (1962) 'The Economic Implications of Learning by Doing', *Review of Economic Studies*, 29, 155–73

ARROW, K. (1983) 'Innovation in Large and Small Firms' in Ronen, J. (ed.) *Entrepreneurship*, Lexington Books, Lexington, 15–28

ARTHUR, W. B. (1994) 'Inductive Reasoning and Bounded Rationality: The EI Farol Problem', *American Economic Review*, 84, 406–11

ARTHUR, B. (1990) 'Positive Feedbacks in the Economy', *Scientific American*, February

BECKER, G. S. (1993) *Human Capital*, 3rd edition, The University of Chicago Press, Chicago

COLEMAN, JAMES (1988) 'Social Capital in the Creation of Human Capital', *American Journal of Sociology*, s95–s120

GOLDMAN SACHS (2000) 'Pharmaceuticals', *Goldman Sachs Investment Research*, 27 January

GROSSMAN, G. M. and HELPMAN, E. (1993) *Innovation and Growth in the Global Economy*, MIT Press, Cambridge, MA

GUZZI, R. and SANGLIER, M. (1997) 'Technological Substitution Effects, with ISIS, a spatial, intersectoral non-linear dynamic model', in Fang, F. and Sanglier, M. (eds) *Complexity and Self-Organisation in Social and Economic Systems*, Springer, Berlin

KALDOR, N. (1961) 'Capital Accumulation and Economic Growth' in Lutz, F. A. and Hague, D. C. (eds) *The Theory of Capital*, Macmillan – now Palgrave, London

KAUFFMAN, S. (1993) *The Origins of Order: Self-Organization and Selection in Evolution*, OUP, Oxford

KAUFFMAN, S. (1995) *At Home in the Universe: The Search for the Laws of Self-Organization and Complexity*, OUP, Oxford

KUZNETS, S. (1966) *Economic Growth and Structure: Selected Essays by Simon Kuznets*, Heinemann, London

MITLETON-KELLY, E. (1998) 'Organisation as Complex Evolving Systems', mimeo, London School of Economics, http://www.lse.ac.uk/LSE/COMPLEX/publications/OACES.htm.

PENROSE, E. (1959) *The Theory of the Growth of the Firm*, Basil Blackwell, Oxford

PENROSE, E. (1985) 'The Theory of the Growth of the Firm Twenty-Five Years After', Uppsala Lectures in Business, University of Uppsala

PRIGOGINE, I. and NICOLIS, G. (1989) *Exploring Complexity*, Freeman, New York

PRIGOGINE, I. and STENGERS, I. (1984) *Order out of Chaos: Man's Dialogue with Nature*, Bantam, New York

PRIGOGINE, I. and STENGERS, I. (1997) *The End of Certainty – Time's Flow and the Laws of Nature*, The Free Press, New York

ROMER, P. (1986) 'Increasing Returns and Long-Run Growth', *Journal of Political Economy*, 94, 1002–37

ROMER, P. (2000) 'Economic Growth' in Henderson, D.R. (ed.) *The Fortune Encyclopedia of Economics*, Warner

ROSENHEAD, J. (2000) 'Complexity Theory and Management Practice', http://www.human-nature.com/science-as-culture/rosenhead.html

SANTOSUS, M. (1998) 'Simple, Yet Complex', *CIO Enterprise Magazine*, April

SCHMOOKLER, J. (1966) *Invention and Economic Growth*, Harvard University Press, Cambridge, MA

SCHULTZ, T. W. (1961) 'Investment in Human Capital,' *American Economic Review*, 51, 1–17

SCHUMPETER, J. (1942) *Capitalism, Socialism and Democracy*, Harper, New York

SOLOW, R. (1956) 'A Contribution to the Theory of Economic Growth', *Quarterly Journal of Economics*, 70, 65–94

STERN, C. W. and STALK, G. (1998) (eds) *Perspectives on Strategy from the Boston Consulting Group*, John Wiley, New York

THALER, R. H. (2000) 'From Homo Economicus to Homo Sapiens', *Journal of Economic Perspectives*, 14, 133–41

Index

115